PAUL VERLAINE

Paul Fearne

All rights reserved, no part of this publication may be reproduced by any means, electronic, mechanical photocopying, documentary, film or in any other format without prior written permission of the publisher.

>Published by
>Chipmunkapublishing
>United Kingdom

http://www.chipmunkapublishing.com

Copyright © 2021 Paul Fearne

ISBN   978-1-78382-6056

PAUL VERLAINE

Readers Note

I have purposely left some grammatical irregularities in the work to give it a fragmented feel.

In the history of literature, we have gone from structured harmony, rhythm and rhyme, to the fragmentation of the modernists.

But what next? Like all good dialectics, we now strive for synthesis of these two modes.
That is why I have left some irregularities in, and taken others out.

In such a manner, we can derive pleasure from structure and technique, but also pleasure from that which is dissonant and fragmented.

The final book, should be in many respects, like a journal full of pencil jottings that retain their errors, such is their charm.

Please enjoy.

Paul Fearne

Verlaine – What of your need to nestle up to the stars, and have your chance at redemption? Be that as it may, there is something here that lets only the best through. We will come again, and see the way to be clear. Can you come again?

The clouds are enough to round us off to sleep. I see your languishing, and know it to be one of hope. You once said poetry was a curse, but let us see about that. There are times in amongst it, we see ourselves for what we really are.

Verlaine – Hoping against hope. Your hospital stays were simply to treat multifarious condi-tions. What you needed was nothing other than the breeze at your back, and a chosen will at your side. Be the strength we have, and there will be an offering.

Watching, as if by need. Calling, without the sense to stop. You had your white angel, and your black angel, and indeed everything in between. But they were your lovers, and your guides. Be that as it may, there were times for freedom, for a sou.

Verlaine – Have you come again? Do you see yourself to be the true and the tried? What is left of all of us, once we have read your life! There are passages in this book that leave us rattled, then we rally, and are relieved at our own life.

There is nothing like this. Nothing in the snow, or on the land. Be the combination of this to that, and yours will be an adventure of vast proportions. Do not sing, the clouds will not stir, and the vacant ash will have no need of the world.

Verlaine – There is in these leaves the sound of the world. And here, where we feel the rounding of things, a new type of soul – one that has no recourse to the wind, nor belief in the suffering of others. There will come a time for release.

You had your demons. You had that which could only make you stay. And then, without thought of your own suffering, a new type of deliverance. One that has chosen you, instead of the other way round. How do we know? We just do.

Verlaine – What have we sought for? What have we known to be true? There is in this mist a solemnity we must not forget. And then, as if by magic, a treasured rhyme, on a sign, and then that which languishes once more. Have your way.

There are things that must not be displayed. Things that must only be read. And here, where the living and the dead ride in mutual harmony, there can be a set course, that has only itself to rubble by. Do not set sail yet – we will be there soon.

Verlaine – Seeing things first, the antechamber is yours. There can only be that which will never fall. And here, where lights do not shine, there is a place for hiding, and a place for letting go. There will be much of that which cannot go.

Most of what is here is porcelain. Most of what is here is above the ground, and not below. There are choices we make, in the midst of life, that harrow the gauge into the night. Do not send yourself on merely placating dreams.

Verlaine – Motion to the stars; feel a heady breath – never look back, always run. And then, when the happenstance of the day runs full circle, there will be a time to say our goodbyes, and gather up our needs, for one last shot.

Caught in the crossfire, you did not want to fight. That is perfectly understandable, indeed. Never measure an arrow by its bow. Always seek redress in the arc.

Verlaine – Be more than two hoverings of the brush. Never see more than we can. There is time here, to be the way. Be the way, and more. What we believed to be sacrosanct, is the marrow of the bone. Do not fight, we will win.

Commiserations, there is only what we need. We will carry on, and know our path to be one not well trod. There are times in amongst it, when the ferry is full to the brim. You went to Eng-land on a number of occasions, with Rimbaud, and then as a tutor.

Verlaine – Casting glances that do not wane. Casting the circumspect with eyes full of fury. Never give a moment's notice. Never win without saying no. Be the lasting, as we are the lips on every sailor. There is no more need here, that is true.

A hardship we should not endure. What is left for the sun, is only ours. Be like minded in be-tween shows. Never give in. Never give in.

Verlaine – Never in a thousand years would I expect you here! But that is okay, is it not, my friend? Be in tune with life, and what will follow will startle a nation. Be the fence, and sitting on it will appear easy. Do not dabble, there is much to do.

And now, forwarding the right address to the right recipient, we come full circle, and know that what comes next is sent to test. The weather is not worn out here, nor the salience of the place a thing to besmirch. What we fought for will take us there.

Verlaine – Never reading, always enjoying. There are times we can never miss. And in those times, there are lots that are never broken. I am here to say thank you. Thank you for your words, your life, and your being. Do not touch, it will stay.

Be the feather, in the dead of night. Be the Trojan when the fields are full. There can never really be a thing to set alight. We will not want it anyway – we are full of the world and her bel-lows. What say you, oh man of treasures – of night time curses.

Verlaine – Ad hoc, and with a vengeance. Never seeing what is in the basket. Never believing for a second that the thing which saves us is the thing that lets us down. Be prepared, the night is not a tender thing. And when the unity of the all persists…then.

Caught on the seam – so much spills. And now that we have come full circle, we see the har-row for the canker, and are more enticed than the thing will bear. I have never seen the day-light – but it is here, and when we sail on, we say - never again.

Verlaine – a choice. Pistols, or the reverberations of time. We choose time.

A new conscience, something of the old. There can never be the thing that waits, awaits in giving, and in solace. Please be attuned to the sun, there is much energy there. Never be retrograde to the toil that weeps. There will be sentience.

Verlaine – Why the tag of demure? Why the nuance to the sleeping giant? Be a hat at the ball – things will come. Be a change in the weather, certainty will arise. And then, when feathers are tarnished, there will be a likeness to the crowd. You will see.

PAUL VERLAINE

All in all, something to see, something to do. Have a raft, and polish it through. Have the mois-ture to fill it taught. And then, when the science of containment reaches the folds of fabric that have no hearse, there will be tears, and then an invective. Yes.

Verlaine – Hang on to your tutelage, there will be malice. Be not the one to bend. Feel your cup between your hands, there will be no visage to weep with. And what I will do now will hearten a soul. Be kind, the misnomer of the wind is fierce.

All the time, there is recompense. It is like the Charlotte and the spice. Be one to trigger a mass, and the light we hide behind, will, like us, be a trend and a solemn feast. Can we mind ourselves afoot? Do not tarry, there is not far to go.

Verlaine - Why are the rivers here so dense? Their density is like ice, and they flow with noth-ing short of abandon. And when the night-time withstands all, there will be flowing in amongst the embers. Be one to envision the cradle – ease will come.

All the more ready. What the belief says to us. There are new things amongst the old that tarry in on the features of the day. I am not one to venture, when the adventure is more like this. Nearing solstice, we say to ourselves – yes, and go again.

Verlaine – Are you the one to say, 'so long', and then hark back to times unseen. What have we thought of, but all that is remiss? What have longed for, but the stars that harry the future? Do not stand again – there will be more time.

And, I say to you, have a rest, and enjoy yourself. Be the temple to the body, and your invigor-ation will give a message to the heart – live and be the thing that winds down to the base. And now, the now, the only thing to say, is simply – 'now'!

Verlaine – Is this the sight I saw one hundred years ago – your body, flying through the aether – and upon in new ways to be, and new oughts to send. Be a wishing, there can be time, and that which she accompanies, will fallow, only for a day.

The soul contains more than the eye. But what diminishes us more than the sight of the whole, is the sight of all the glad tidings that baste in ovens untold. There are more ways to feel than we ever thought possible. And here, we will come again.

Verlaine – are you arrested once again? Do not scale the ramparts for a fashioning in silk, there is more to love, than ever was felt. I am here for you, in ways untold. Never sing your name in the message or the tie. There will be love, and fruit.

Message me up, and let me find a way through. Be careful, I will use you to scale my crimson neverness. Be a linen, and folds in ancient garb will come in streams.

Verlaine – The savagery of your partition into life is more than a send from times untold. I knew you once, all those years ago. I knew your soul, a thing that knew the taste of it. Be a rain to my roadside, and here we will find new ground.

A little bit of sideways movement is the thing that will get us there. A beauty it seems is laugh-ing the hay down. When we see ourselves again, here the lights are on, and when we finally figure out what the blaze is for – here there will be something to eat.

PAUL VERLAINE

Verlaine – Your shimmering amounts to much more. Your vertiginous nature harks the swallow and the bean. A left hand lug, never a mirror in the swine. There can only be one outcome. One outcome to lather by. And here, a new way.

Confounding those who laugh, confounding those who don't. There are means to ends untold. The mist moves through the trees, and the sun does its dance through the clouds. Will we sing again through the borrows, and through the hills.

Verlaine – Being the fill of things. Being what temporality can only guess at. Being what are the most treasured of times. We see ourselves now, as we never have before. It is the light we see when we have an inkling for the rest.

We love every moment of the time we have left. We sense another era beginning, another new way to be. Do not hear the vision of ourselves, as we encumber the nation with straddles of complacency. Do not ring dear, we will see.

Verlaine – Are you the ghost who sits in the chair of tomorrow, or has your demand on things given rise to verisimilitude? We do not know, nor can we feel. There are things here that rise to the pinch, and knowings that only rise at bedtime.

Come and be a part of the greatest adventure of all – world literature. There are more things now than laughter can away. Be the stereotype, and yours will be the legend and the curse. Be what may, there is no time like the now.

Verlaine – obtuse, and needing. Holed away in the sempiternal. Be all that we can be, and so much more. What is left of the range? We will see. There comes a chance at togetherness, and that chance has now gone. Oh well.

Estranged from life, we hear button on silk. We hear the life we had, and that was more than enough. Be a vapour in a languorous sky. Be a tune on the lips of the sea. And hear, more than ever, hear what has to be said. Be vulgar, and then, a dance.

Verlaine, there is a test here – there is a test to seal the most ardent passions. Be in the mould, and yours will give unction to distant dilapidations. Be the stranger mass, and the signposts will have their way. We are not here to sense the song.

Resting in the wings, the detriment is shown the door. And now, fixing wings made of snow, we fly the flight of the mistletoe. And have the sense to nestle in close. Do not close the door, there is light still to be had – and we will have it!

Verlaine – upper and beyond, through, and in pieces. What we thought was the edge of things is a store in wintery blast. Longed for, and smitten – and, indeed trestled.

Handsome, and in need of a trim – what did they say, about your looks? Never the eagle, al-ways the swimming of the length. Distraction, and pitiful revere. What is left, is the dust on fin-gernails and in disquietude. Be the last to stand. Just bring.

Verlaine, according to the semblance, there is no mass to be merry by, nor feather to wrench to safety. Be at your leisure, and see yourself as a resting noon after a grand feast. There can only be more of the sound of treasures in autumnal light.

A light in the distance, that much is said. A light in the marrow, never before. What we said, cannot be undone, no matter how much we prise our fingers from on top. A lifetime of birches, new steel, and an unction of servitude. This will cover us.

Verlaine – it was said of you, you were weak in all things, all things except poetic creation! An apt epitaph, if ever there was one. What else can we say about you, Prince of Poets? We will say yes to life, and then the danger really starts!

Rest in the vestibules, and then let them arch. The noise is like a slamming gate. There is a turgid sound that hallows in noisome delectation. The wind will come as ice knows the solemnity. Ring by degrees, there will be a place for us.

Verlaine – what is this? We come and see ourselves in the formative stages, and there is the wing. A wing, and a tail, and all that has come to burst a stretched face. There can be no more, and that which is not will follow us. Here we are.

Wishing for hearts, that spectate on roller hills. There is time that functions in the way of things. There is a place in amongst it, that hides no arbour. Be a wind through the arcs, and the size of your compunction will not be belittled. Come and dash.

Verlaine – are you alive? Are you the one to be in the midst of it? There are things we must not relinquish, at all costs. There are things we must always do, that matters no silence. Be mine, oh wind, oh solace, and the treasure will be yours.

On road step, on holler. There is a place in the silence. A place that hinges on well-springs of life. Be a change, in amongst changes, and the listening will be yours. Can you see the wind? Can you knock back the levity of the situation?

Verlaine – is this what you seek? Is this the way forward? We can always sense things in the right, down below, in step with time. Be a wastrel, and yours will be the might of day. Come to believe in things once again. Yes, come.

All the more reason to be. All the more reason. Hanging through the horizon, like a feeling we never had. A disguise that leaves us tentatively, like a rainbow down the knack. There are places here that do not relinquish. Do not say, when.

Verlaine – Sense cannot curtail us. Moisture in the trees cannot be a belated gift. What is here, will always be here. What has come, has never been. Be the sky, and the clouds will entertain us. There is something new in all of us.

Sophisticated, and pronounced. Being in love with the moment. All that is reckoned, is reck-oned in salt. Be a believer, in a believers realm. And when you do, sing.

Verlaine – there are no steps to take, from here to there. There is only the vine, and all that she has. Be a sculpture made of marble, and yours will be a keepsake. Be the mess left behind, and the silence will not follow you. Dream a deep dream.

Coming, and going, seeing what is next. There is a sign in the wind that has no wish to send unto sleepless byways. And when we leave a trail in the sand, we leave it for you. And now, I will hazard a guess, that what is left is not yours, nor mine. Yes.

Verlaine – you tried your hand at farming, with the parents of your lover, but you were not that good. Sometimes things work for the better in the market of stars. And here where life adjusts itself, a new sort of things comes from nowhere!

Forests that keep stationary. Inclement weather that is no bother. There is here a sort of heart, that does not beat, but only believes itself to be a wraith in wraith's attire. There is a fondness for the night and all she brings. Yes, all she brings.

Verlaine – a new set of shoes for you. A new way to be accompanied. What is this? What is this demure? It is us, as we fight for the lattice, that has no build. We have come for something, but what is the sand that harrows in the chosen silk?

Complaining, never more so than now. But we must only sense the dilapidation in more than a test. There are ways, and there are ways. The hope we have that the sand is viscous. And now, a sound that delights. We will listen, and know quietude.

Verlaine, a handsome interweaving, of this to that, of up to down, of around to now. Please be faithful, I have known much strife. There is a likeness in the way of things, there is now a cre-scendo of belief that carries me forward. Yes, and then?

Opening up to the dawn. Having that which does not curtail. There is a belief in the wind that the solstice is never a carrier of bad news. Be a light in the darkness, and sense with play across the stage of love. And then, a new way.

Verlaine – a carrying on, that disrupts the play. Do not be alarmed, there is more to come. There is now only one way forward, and it comes to us in guises unknown, and unblemished. We will not have the way blocked by anything, or anyone.

A slight catch at the seam of things. What we must do now, is expend our talents in their cho-sen directions. And here, where the silence does not beckon, there will be a chance at skyward motion, and an eavesdropping on the edge of things.

Verlaine, and what we call next. Be the thing which tramples in the corner of existence, and then without a care, new found hope, and a desire to see our souls by the bannister. Here, oh here, there is relief, and a touch of motion through the sky.

Foraging, and seeing new time. We will not touch what is left. And here where the sand is in the hourglass, a new time will be made, and sent to the washroom to dry the glades of so much. But what must we do now? We must fathom deeply.

Verlaine – we must see each other again, for one last time, and then, let go, and then back again. See which way is enough, and then decide on clippers together.

The little bit of umbrage we feel at life, has never really left us. And here where the distance does not stroll, there is a further way to be. Do not be alarmed! The bell which intercedes in things has long since diminished – and now, what next?

Verlaine – a wholesome pledge to stand upright. There is more than the last gasp which is left. There is more than the harrowing of the meadow. There is us, and all we have at our call. Be the song in the manger, and there will be simpler verse.

Ongoing, and through – there can be no more of this than a trick of the eye. I rest, and am pla-cated. Do not hear me, I am one to shout. There are things I cannot do, but there are things I am not alarmed at. Be what may, we will come.

PAUL VERLAINE

Verlaine – is the weather fine enough for you? Are your clothes in keeping with the times? I have had more than this in dreams of long time sagely reminiscences. Be a coach in the mire – be a salience where hope fears to tread. There will be enough.

Going against the grain, is something we should all explore. It is now time to shake off the vast array of temperatures that do not exhibit any trait but this. And here, where tasks are done in halves, a belief that once through, we will never depart.

Verlaine – there is no time like this one. No time like this one to send our feathers, into outer realms, and have them come back through the night. Even here, we sense that what is here, will always be. Never come back. Never come back.

In the outmost cropping, there lies a place, that has no place. In it, there is a wind that has as its insistence the shark and the mire. Do we settle the language in the steam of things? I should hope not. We are there to entice, and never to leave.

Verlaine, are you the station, that has only the mile? Are you envisioned in great gaiety, a measure that winds as it patrols? There can only be the wind at our backs. And then, without a thought, nor care, there believes something else to tremble.

And then, in the meaning of the rhyme, there is a conscious trick. It tricks as it wanders through, and has as the means a sort of fashion that kindles no lead. And there, in the in-between of things, height, and a semblance of coal.

Verlaine – are you the wanderer, that night cannot dark? Are you the seething that has as a launch the evening cascade of starlit distance? There is much here that is worth investigating, but we will see unto the end, and see where things lead.

Afterwards, there is calm. Afterwards from the great crescendo, there is noise that has only forgiveness. We will know our time to envision such despair, it is not now, nor even in the sky, a whole moisture in the trimmings and out.

Verlaine – sense what I am seeing. Sense the ablutions that only pale. There is more here than can be seen. There is more like a hole in the tenacity of fall. We will not believe our selves like the arc and the meaning of things unsaid. Be with it.

And now, where the dire and the sundry all perplex, there is a moisture in the half light, that does not see ourselves in the one thing that we can stop.

Verlaine – is your flight the way of all strangers? Is this where we are led? I know that, in the daylight, our reticence is large. But be true, and the white of the sense of it will not curse us. There is time still – time to envisage a semblance of the dark.

Do not hold on. But only let go when you are ready. There is a chance here, to do something around the mark, and stay withheld amongst the dark. In this we are free. In this we are free. I will not think again. I will only think again. Yes.

Verlaine – and here, where life is of the harvest, there is a close call with the wind that will open the doors for something larger. What can this be, I am inclined to believe. Do not scent that wood, it is scented enough. It is wood. That is plain.

An open door; we look in, and there we are, darkness. Where is the light? There is none. Where is the sound? There is none. Can we only find ourselves in the dark? I guess there can be no other way. We will not famish. We will only grow taller.

Verlaine – are you still drinking? Is that your lot, to be the one who never tethers, nor launches at the stable door? There is a well for you that contains within itself all that vestiges of unknown origin feel. And here a moral sign, of cross lettered temperance.

What of the nous? What of the sensibility to rise in test and fire? There is a licence here to be in charge of accessibility, and be the tune that every sea has ever whistled. Do not cling on, there will be no more draft, and no more of the nice.

Verlaine – are you hidden; behind hills of intransigence. There are no more falls, nothing more to laden the thickets with. But maybe, in distressing lack, there is new need, and fathomless abysses to feel upon. Where are we all now?

Catching sight of the rainbow, there comes a wish to be as we are, in a sense to be who we want to be. There is like so much, to sense and to find, to see, and to rectify. Will we laugh, but never again like this. Feel free, they are numbered.

Verlaine – the want is in you, and can never be without. Are you without? Do you sense the need we have to gather the rose petals of the aplomb and see them fall right before our unbe-lieving eyes? I will see your eyes, and raise you a farm.

There are fragrances that have no loop. And in this lies the shell of weak despair, and then, without the being made to shelter, there comes a feeling that is like no other. This no other is a sound that cannot be encapsulated by anyone!

Verlaine – you have settled the score. Yes, you have been there, and given rice when there was no more to give. What of the sun-dance, that has no wheels to pull, nor distance to wane? Be a likening through the woods, we will stand a chance.

And now, we go. And now we levy half full, and full of yoke. Do not despise me, I am of the tangent, of the steel, of the way we live, and the way we go. There can only be the simplest of things – this much I know. There will only be the now. Yes.

Verlaine - of the flight, there seems new need to risk by, and now, when we thought ourselves a farthing, we will not be one to catch a cold, nor be the whole that divides.

What is missing, is not you – is not the life; is not the saying. It is all of these things, and more. Do not seem to us everything you are not, there are templates to go by, and all that is written. Be a ramshackle base in a land of windows and traits.

Verlaine – there exists a place that is no place; a land that is no land. In this place, in this land, there is a wind – a wind that hatches no plot and wheedles no dimension. There can only be a sound to accompany this wind – the sound of bent birches.

And now, a wish; a wish to wit-curdle, and something more besides. There is a new style to want to be, a new fake to arrest the aperture, and now, what we thought was a science is monsoonal gloom, is now the light that guides the way!

Verlaine – Factoring in the very heart of the space, there seems nothing new to venture by, nothing overt to sense the notion by. And here, where we lounge, a set of repartee's to rac-quet around. There is moisture in the air – it will suffice.

All the more reason to be, just here, just now. There is likely a wonderful grade of silk to keep us company, and then, once we have let go, new tassels to guard against the fire – the fire that has no steam. Believe in us; this is not the end, just the start.

Verlaine – we seek you out. We seek you in. We have the nails of the board to awaken you. You are a shell-fish, to guard hole against. There is a mark that does not leave, nor is men-tioned in the annuls of time. We will see things afresh.

Catch something out of mid-air. There is time, still time. I have heard it said the rain on a tin roof is like the air we breathe, and the sunlight here, a god-send. Be in tune with the life, and something magical will happen! What is that thing? We are unsure.

Verlaine, I hear you say, Verlaine! There is much to be said, and much to be undone. But that is fine in the accoutrements of the day – and the daylight? Shall we sink to the bastion of air, and the Tuesday of the soul? Yes, in time we must, that is so.

What is there left? What is the semblance like? There feels a solemn grasp. Solemn in the sense of the wind. Do not lie here waiting, the table is not straight. It will only fall, and leverage for our fate. There is like nothing else here. This much. Yes.

Verlaine – Verlaine! Are you the tangent – the twilight, and the bone? Do you curse blood red, and then hurry home? This much is sure, we will run until running forgets itself in silence and regret. Silence and regret, and all things. Yes.

A catch in the sky, woven in silk. Woven in destiny, woven in time. Do I hear the daylight, as it crinkles through stain-glass in an abandoned abbey at first light? We will come for you again. We will come for the right time, and all that she gives.

Verlaine – are you sensible; do you bleed red? Is the life of it on the edges of what is possible? We have learnt a valuable lesson watching you these past days – and that lesson is to see straight, act right, and be left, and then, without a care, twirl.

And there we are – a nice and sundry place, where time cannot go, where the sun is at an ebb, and the channel of the furnace is not what we expect. Listen, it will be you.

Verlaine – are you the semblance of the night? Do you come in scenes unending? There is a chance, amongst all, to see things anew. Be a fallen warrior, and the lost will be yours. I don't doubt you are coming – will I see you? There must be time.

A vista, a vista that awaits. There is merriment here, like the far and the gone. I will not linger long, it will not suit. And here where the clouds do not move, a sundry space, that has as its initial tumult the wings of guided stallions. We will wait.

Verlaine – are you a messenger, a messenger from the beyond? Does life find you simply in-creasing, and not decreasing? I will not find the licence to travel to places undefined. Be what may, there can never be a song greater than this. Be what may.

Rimbaud, have you found him again, just for the sake of it? Does your wrist partake of silence? Can you once again swing? They all ask, could he still write? What does the sound have to say? There is a belief in things, but what of this?

Verlaine – there is now the leaning of a vine that comes to the foam on an ancient sea. The colour of it mesmerises. It is June, to our November! Gusts of wind blow in ancient memory. I cannot see you again – but what of this? I will find a way.

Forests, and closed memories – fortresses of pure abandon – reckless abandon. There is now something slight in the wind that has brought us here. It is the shackles of the future, and all that will come to pass. I can hear your rattling, and raise you!

Verlaine – are you the one to wince? At every fibre, and every salient window, there is a fabric that guides the way. Have no fear, Verlaine, there can be no more of the levity upon light that structures! Have we found the way – we have.

In the silence, a great boon is born. In the driving rain, there is a feeling of respite. I know how to reckon the forces of persistence, as they spill once again down the curb side in the snow. What will we find at the end of it all? Something great.

Verlaine – is this your stark reminder? Is this what you have found? I have found my way, why not you for yours? All you need do, is find out how to move backwards. This is the key, wouldn't you say? But now, all the riding is upon us – quick.

What is there left? – I have no feeling for it. What is there to do? – I will come again. There are forces at work with the pulse. Be attuned, poet, be attuned, and know that the simplicity of the stars is in all of us. This is all we can say, all we can feel.

Verlaine – do you see now? Do you come in splendour when your back is bent in harvest? Do you know how to envision the life of it now that it is empty? There can only be what there is, and nothing more – each to their own.

A courtesan, and belief in the journey. At odds, and then resplendent. I will sing to you, and have my sound carry back. Are you the tether, the tether to the harmony. Do not strike a bow, it will be in vein. There is here amusement. So come.

Verlaine – what do we give? What do we give, so that our pulse remains intertwined? There is nothing in the middle of this that seems so apt.

 What has the wind to say? What have we, the lost and wind swept, seen? What have the no-tions that we are free ever painted? There is now a time to see what the traveller sees. And then, when the danger has passed, a reckoning, and a new way.

Verlaine – do you believe in the way forward? Do you see it as a chance, and not a lasting abyss? There are signs that the past has taken much, but also, that the future will never give in. Do not see the horizon, it is covered in silk. Be that as it may, yes.

What has been so strong here, is the fibre of a rope that has no twine. No cannons to loosen, no distance to swine. Perhaps there is something new here? Something that catches the sunlight in a lasting tribute. I am glad I stayed for the ride!

Verlaine – There is a thing we call the distance, and it is here. There is this thing we call the way, and it is here. There can never be the strength of a thousand ships to out-reach our care. Be the whistling on the shore line, and the wind will play its part.

Can we see ourselves once again in times of trouble, times of ease. There is a new found longing that has as its vice a grip that knows only the invectives of steel. Be the semblance of something larger, something not of this place nor time.

Verlaine – there is now a new found conditioning that makes the strength of our forbears en-larged. Do not be one to see the sun, it can only hurt the ones we love. I will tell you a strange story, it will be the way of things – yes. We come to this place.

On the coast of so much, on the dreams of a thousand wild men. And here where we linger to the day, there is found a laughter that has not the science of the times. Be integral to the sea, as yours will be life in amongst it. There, we have seen.

Verlaine – I have come. I have come for you, and your need. I will not let go until the rain has subsided. All this makes sense now. All this dew on the ground, that was never once there, never once! There can be a place that harbours, and we will find it.

A witness to history, that has no lesson. A feeling we had, that does not know itself. There are mitigations that do not sour, and long lasting friendships that stand any test. I will have for you a pleasure and a boon, and all that will be.

Verlaine – you have your say, and then, let us have ours. There is a time for being true. There is a well-spring that gives our hearts away. There is a fathom to the coil, and then back again. Treat us write, and the soil will have no more of us.

The vagabond, and the treatise. There is not enough to sing by. There is now what the moon will not steal. Have the way forward cast in bronze, and that scar will be appeased. Come for-ward, my one, you are free, and you have the key.

Verlaine – the distance brings with it rain, but more than that, a heavy mist, one that is hard to see through. But we will see through it, and into the belonging, and then out again. There is a rhyme that will not burst, for any of the worst.

Catching on, and seeing it through. Being the remainder in a distant land. There can only be one thing to do, and that is look up from our easel, and wait!

Verlaine – in the haste of it, have we left our souls at the door? In this way we live, and so die. There are nuances that let through the light of the mind. We cannot save the castings of worn out silk, but what we can do, is find the time to be, once again.

There are places in the middle of life that have only the newness of a side born intransigence. And here, where the night is like a viper, an old type of crises does not fathom the guile of all out incumbency. What have we said that requires no want?

PAUL VERLAINE

Verlaine – do you see the treasured belief – is it here, like in times of outstanding constancy? There is now, no turn on the horizon, no belief worth giving. There is here now the obstacle and not the chase. Be in the manner of things, we will be sturdy.

Coming up for much needed air, the vacuum of the structure has an all-out mesmerising con-tainment! There is like the never before seen wave that we all are a part off. And then, when we least expect, something of great compunction.

Verlaine – do you remember your vagabond life? It ended with the generosity of friends and admirers. But do you wish for the sun to rain down on you with fits and starts. Do not be a lark in a tempest filled sphere. There will be things to say.

Come and be the placard to a life. Come be the new sun, to an old deity. There are things we must not see, things we must only do. I will chase the prerogative to the centre of life, and then nestle things away like time itself. We will away.

Verlaine – are you the one to stand on shards unmoving? Does your movement catch the sense we have to stay at liberty? And now there is life at the end of the visage, and a whet-stone to fill the void. Do not worry, we will come.

Counting backwards, we see ourselves in times of clay. That which we do with it, is ours for the taking. Be intrusive, in an intrusive land, and all that will be, is the silk between our fingers. Come and see the play, it will leave you resplendent.

Verlaine – this is the way we go. This is ours for the need and the song. Do not be the one to see the light shine through your hair. There will be a way forward, through all, and through all else. Come, we are wanting of you.

Come, and be the heart I know you can. And then, without the Trojan in our steps, there will be a likeness to the sea, and a new way to be. What is there now? A look to the tempting of plates awry. This much is our solemn harp. This much.

Verlaine – A feeling we once had that life will see the way, and shine on tresses unbidden. There is here a sense of the right, and of the now and of the simplicity, of all, and of nothing. There can only be the sharpest of turns. Yes, indeed.

What has become cast in grey, that does not linger in a grand muse. There is a simplicity of the journey as it comes about in ancient wonder. There is never a time to see the fashioning of cards from the daylight to the night.

Come for the sound, and not the crest of oceans wild. There is white here.

Verlaine – there is a substance that is not of this earth. It makes the trees grow, and the rain come. As poets, it is in us as we sleep. And when we awake, and create, there this substance gets used, and we embolden the possibilities of what can be.

There is now not the slightest chance of renouncing upon the seas of fate. And here, where we come to the shallows like they never were, we will find ourselves again, in the joy that is the meaning between all things. Do not see it otherwise.

Verlaine – Coming into contact with all things precious, we know that the wind will have only the arrangement in time to a chosen few. Be the placard, that has a picture of you and I, and this will convert our feelings from dust to dapper.

Sounding out the seasons like they were the accompaniment to the dawn. Your face belies your pen, but what of that! There is more to talk about here than we expected. Live the life, and see how you are treated. See the falcon for the moon.

Verlaine – What is there in the district of the heart? Your heart sung with your first love. The poems you wrote to court her, where perfection themselves. You tore no beat until Mathilde left you, but that is a story for Rimbaud, and another time!

A lying down, that has no face to hide. A wishing that opens new vistas. A hole to the pants that brings a bitter truth. Be the warrior of the warriors caste, and the rain you feel will be enough to see you through. A condolence that leaves us breathless.

Verlaine – are you in love with the clouds? Do you settle on things untimed? Is this the way we find new things? There is a distance between this and that desire, that almost has us at a grasp. Never see the furnace for what it is, it will only burn.

There is a timely acceptance, that never leaves a vault. I have found us crouching with things undone, but that is no way to see the change. There is a likeness here, with the crowd of many. Do not see us as we are, there will be further time.

Verlaine – is this the way to live? Is this the way? Do we spend time on rooftops, to see the rain come? I will only envision one thing more, and that is that the stage is now upright, upright with life. Do not single others out, they will not come.

And when we say we are dilapidated, this is what we mean. And here where we find ourselves once again, there will be a repugnant insistence that has no way forward, and no way back. Do you see for yourself the harshness of the way forward.

Verlaine – there is now a sense that things will right themselves, unto the life, unto the tundra! And when we take that second look into the mirror, what shall we find, but a landfall that is tentatively a sea-fall. There are things we must not see.

And then, what of the life? What of the sand bar of which we speak? Is this where we find ourselves, once again, in lieu, and in tempest blast? There is a sound we must fashion, fashion into things made of wood. And when we are done, a new feeling.

Verlaine – caught on your regal loft, there is much more to find. Much more to see, and much more to do. There we are, and there we find ourselves.

The touchstone of the waters do surely intrigue us. And here where the tightness of the fibre of things is more than we could have grasped, there will come a time for great passage, and timeless chances. Do nothing more, there can be only this.

Verlaine – the weeping we do, to vary the interlude, is enough to have us stalk the bray shire all in one motion. And here, where the love we feel for the night is not enough to placate the rest of us, we see. And here we are then, with hop and step.

I have felt the wind move beneath me. I have felt more than my fair share. And then, when the night encompasses growth, there will be a timing to stave off time itself. And when we swear a solemn oath, we will come around that one more time.

Verlaine – the adding to the scene, is not what we had in mind. But that is enough to silence our woes, and give heart to our beating. Where must we live, to truly be ourselves? Do we live and die in a place worthy of souls?

The spring is here! And we are at a repartee, one that only sings at the grasp of merriment. Do not change course, I hear you say! There is time enough for the lightning to crash. And now a feeling like the wind has come, and will never return.

Verlaine – are you the one to train on new ground. New layers of the permanent to wind back. New wisdoms to reach toward. New feelings to detail in full. What we had was not the landing, but the sea was not rough that day. Be not alone.

The message to be relayed does not embark upon the want. It arcs and treasures through the sky, like a semblance made of rye. Be the one who delivers, and yours will be a keepsake. There is no time to be as we truly want. Yes, no time.

Verlaine – do you see the way through, as a trim through the parchment? Is this the way to say, olay? Do we hark back to stranger times, that have no beat to muster, nor replenishment to believe? This much we can be sure of.

A gorge that does not diminish. A sense of the beauty of things. There is here, in this land, a motion to be understood, before the very fibres of the arc – a further motion that travels through the sky, and through the wasteland. Come what may.

Verlaine – what we have here is never like what we had – but that is okay, and through the day, we find ourselves a winning seal, that all it does is leech water through an ingrained pipe, and says to us all – be there.

Hanging on to fate – we laugh again, but at what? We sense new fibres at the gates. New senses of what is real. And then, like a shallow sand, that provides some resistance, a special embrace that has as its tiles the dust of a century.

Verlaine – A new foundling, found and not forgotten. What we though had the viper as trail, is now the moon shine through the mist. And then a sort of release, that has no need of need in tempest bright. Come, and be the one who sweats.

A case of the trying to be calm in a very busy situation. This much belies the caste, and has as its tail the looking glass eye. There are windows never to be seen.

Verlaine – are you the heart? The heart and the stone. Does your head proliferate in outstanding verse still – 'he never wrote a bad line'. And then without compunction, so said the man. There are trails forthwith, and outside of. Never going back.

There are changes in the wind that have neither the salt to shade, nor the merriment to have done. There are ranges that do not speak, and passage ways that have the solitude of mass. There are new types of wisdoms here – handed down. Yes.

Verlaine - What is at a loss, is not the loss of sages, who are truly missed, but the loss of those barbarians at the gate, who never once patrolled a thing. Do the wildest of places securely meet our needs, and then hang down in longing, for the faintest?

Have the need to ride high, and revoke your contumely, in spirit at least. Be the best hedge, the worst of which is the bravado that echoes through the hatchling. But what is beyond, the this and the that - the heart and the swallow, and all that comes.

Verlaine – do you speak of conquests, in a mighty cauldron of love and fear? Is this the motion we have – that of always being forward? There can be no greater love than this – to partake of the word, and see in play, figurehead to so much. Yes.

The notion of the simplicity is implied in the speak ease command of the hardships of the wanderer, who without camaraderie, forseeks the noon day sun, to which, in lingering solitude, there is, a new way to be. Come what may.

Verlaine – what is this we seek? What are the wishes that land on solemn ground? There are new tidings that have as their want all the seasons of the sea. Do not transgress against the fibre of the life, there can be nothing else. This much is clear.

A new way to swim, where swimming is not an arc above the rest. And here, where the lines and latitudes of the moisture cannot wear us down, there is a wanting that has no voice, and no sense to be. We will aspire to this place, you and I.

Verlaine – happiness is the ingot we seek, but what of the rest? What of the rest of life, as she seeks once again for the timing in the nomenclature. Be a rising tide, and the sun will not burn you. Be the water in the rock pool and the days will come again.

Fishing for life. Fishing for the early signs of what has gone before. And then, when the fash-ioning of a rainbow will not have the day, there is a trump in the air, that has no vice, no means to be, nor sequence to carry. Will we see the plain for what it is?

Verlaine – hanging on, until the vestiges of the night are no more. We will sing now as if thought itself has vanished. And then when we are through, a new way! But do not lose the action, it does not do to spoil. And then, without a care...

Catching all that is catchable. Not seeing the reef for the shore. Being harassed to a point that is not containable. There is not something that can only be described in guessings. But that is okay, there can only be what we seek, and seek and then find.

Verlaine – a message from the beyond. You are wanted in seeds of silk, seeds of grass. There is never anything more to find here, never anything more to see.

There is in here, the sounds of treasures laden. The treasure is your treasure, your words, as they came from a part of you that did not know this world. There is never anything more we could say, more than this – more than the world!

Verlaine – is this your measure, the measure of a man? Can we not see the aspect of the flight for what it is? Do we succumb to the strictures of the night, before the gambler in us reckons the clause? Do this and we are left fight blind – yes.

Come with the motion of all the stars, and we will be in tune with much. Come and be the rav-ages of time, and the silk in us will find new beds to lay on. There is now a feather in step, and in time, with all that is. Be the languid, and all will be yours.

Verlaine – has what you've been given, taken away your surprise? Has the night you found hastened your delivery? When did you find time to write, my Verlaine? Was it in between sips? In between motions that had no motion? Do what you will!

Gaining in renown, your life spent itself in often frequented hospital beds, for a myriad of conditions. But your poetry lived on, and on, until you could no more. There was never anything more to it than this, suffering and acclaim.

Verlaine – was there a reason for your disrupture, my Verlaine? Do the things which carry us forward, also carry us backward? Is the seething mass a thing of world tiding? The vault is near enough, let us jump into reams of sodden mass – Yes.

And there, in the midst of it, a silence that has sense to bring. And then, when the daylight comes afresh, there will be inside of us a reckoning that has only steel to be, and solitude to languish by. There is always something here – always something.

Verlaine – the test we have to settle old scores is enough, in the end, to break brittle bones. And then, when the night sheds her accompaniment, there is in the well-stone that which is like no other. The distance is cried, as the life is made to sear.

Having further mischief through the dawn, the tentacles of remorse do not bother us. And then, as if by magic, the solitude of the sun is like a thing never born. And when we have had our fill, a new source to accompany the old. Now, here we go.

Verlaine - are we against the fibres of the very articulated bastion of the well-spring? Does this type of thing not hold us back? This is excitement lived, and nothing will still us. Be the troubadour, and yours will mix. Be the things that listen. Yes.

And then, when things have settled, a newly arrived stasis will descend. And here, where the light does not breathe, a belief that the sunlight has, to keep on going, and never lose track. There is the sun here to guide its rays. But nothing more.

Verlaine – the soldier in all of us, has the night of a feather, a feather to rest upon the ledge. Be the means to achieve your goals, and what you will find will startle you. What have we said, but all. What have we found, but all. What have we seen? Yes.

After the daylight has receded, a new type of drive. One that has the merriment of the ages to see as its betterment, and elongation. Here we are then, alone again!

Verlaine – are you alive? Do you sweat in darkest times? Is all that remains of you a stifling mix of memories. No, we have your words, that translate into life – so you live! Yes you do. And so, in amongst it, you swelter through fire and ice.

Catching the harbour for all she is worth, and listening for the lane to have the sense to lay. And now we are there. Now we have the chance to breathe that deeper breather. The journey was not easy, but these things never are. Be alive!

Verlaine – When you reckon things are sugar coated, how much of the life is for the sand, and how much for the wayward? There is a new way to be free! A new way to bear the burden of the steeple, and have it wriggle on close, more close than ever.

Never before have the sands of the hour glass moved so freely – never before have the trees blown to their base with such abandon. And in this motion there winds a silver track, that has no need of the time, or all that shall be married to her.

Verlaine – in the middle of it – do you see the course, and do you run it for mere sport. Let us breathe again, and have our breath mosey on up the middle, so that songs that have no har-bour do not miss a beat. There will be more to come.

A fledgling that has no time to rest. No time to be at one with its surroundings. But what of the rest of life? There is only time, time for what is best. Give life to the beating of sombre wings, and here, the semblance is one of ever after.

Verlaine - And there, in the wind, where we cannot see so clearly, there is a fence, and on that fence, is a rope. On the rope there is a mouse, and in that mouse there is life, and in this life, is the wind, where we cannot see so clearly…

And here, where we cease to be wanderers, and take up merriment against our oppressors, there will be flight amongst the eagles, and as they land, new dimensions to commute, and new ways to be, and be solitary.

Verlaine – do you see now, the life and the bones. Do you see now that which has a heart. Do you hesitate to write, when writing is all that encompasses the dawn. Do not shout here, there is only time for quick silence. There will be more time.

A vast expanse, of things, and apparatus, new feelings to let fly, and all that will be. Vast ex-panses, yes. And now there will be a tune on lips of the sea. But why do we come? There is only one answer to that – we come to fathom to the very bottom.

Verlaine – do you sleep? Do you envision once again? Envision all that has come to pass, and all that will be? There is more time here to know. More time than the vastness of it. Why do we not come when times are straight? We do not know.

A glass that cannot be seen through. The only substance that can be seen through it, is the dawn's light. And then, only a sliver of it comes. This is the way of it, for us all. If we can turn ourselves into the light of the dawn, here, we would pass.

Verlaine – come and be a gentleman in gentleman's quarters. Come and see the wave of it in the corner of our eyes. There is a new found lease on it.

And then the merry-go-round speeds, and the aplomb of the occasion needs no rest. And when we see things afresh, there is a moisture that does not rise, only to vanish in the air of the old. There, where hearts are like fires, darts are as vanquish foes.

Verlaine – come and see the sequined attire, it matters not what the loudest sound will do. Be a measure of the man, and see us all fall. Be by the wayside, and then through the way we came. There is never any reason to rise, only this.

Getting closer and closer, closer to the centre. The centre of an all-out belief. And then, when the mention is a fallacy, we will linger again in the night-time embrace, that can give only what has been gotten. And here, a new way to be.

Verlaine – are you one to trod on winter trails, full of snow and ice and the freezing of the not-withstanding? There is here a shallow lyre that does not sense the infraction. I will not see for it myself, in amongst everything that has already gone on.

Constantly arising, for all the sounds of the world. There is now a saying, that does not live on in renegade form. It is the last of old race, that harks back to ancient wonders, and even older steel. And then when we catch the last ship – Yes.

Verlaine – is yours the steeple to each rendezvous? Is this the way forward through the mist? Can we see a motion in the clouds, a motion that was not there before? This is like an old in-sight, passed from parent to child, over the generations.

Like a moon that does not float. Like a trail that is too well hidden. And then, without care, nor rhyme, nor reason, a flippancy that buoys the last thing we see. But what of the transparency of the surge? What of the now, and all she will develop?

Conscious of the lack of the need in this place, there lies a dangerous pool. In it swim the gar-goyles of respite, and what it means to be on the plain of ill-repute. Do, always as you wish, but keep yours and mine separate, until the drenching of a fast.

Verlaine – The cost, what of it. The cost of sun embarked seekers, theirs is the never ending realm, where the classic sits beside the modern – the symbolist and the chaser, wringing down in ancient wonder, that has no the course of all that is.

Everlasting, and then a kind of new invective to pass the old. There is a time for all this, that has not the turn of speed, nor the left and right partitions that steel the resolve. I have seen the way forward, it is like the cradle and the hay.

Verlaine – a different sort of eddying, where each eddy blows a new sound, and doesn't stop to weep, any more than is usual at least. Caught in the register of tiny waves that have the de-cency to stop the mill, and break the need down.

Having the sense to blow wood, and know it to be a thing un-hastened. Be the sight, and yours will be the landing. Be what is sure, and strength will follow like a moonlit promenade. There is something more we must mention – we dig for gold.

Verlaine – are you the one who knows how to come forward, even despite the ravens call? Are you the dust that does not settle? Is this where we stand, cheek to cheek? And in line to a vision, there can still be song, and a little respite.

Never a smaller thing has entered the manor at this time. And then, without care nor com-punction, a midnight interlude that leaves us breathless. I will not stand the likes of it again. Never in this life nor the next. I am want to see things this way.

PAUL VERLAINE

Verlaine – come, my prince, my Prince of Poets. We will away until the vestiges of sand that keep us here are gone. And then, when we land, we do so with coquetry envisioned, and all that comes in the night. Be a sense never to see us rise again.

Forging ahead, there is never any distance from here to the stars. I sound so weak, but am so strong. There is a life raft here that has saved a thousand souls. Do you believe in fate? You must, you must, you must move forward, and through and up.

Verlaine – This much I will tell you, the doors do not sleep, as the shrouds do not encumber. In the middle of a song so lavish, the betterment of the world can wait. And then, without the need to diminish the solstice, a breaking of chains - Freedom.

Verlaine – a new sight, one that does only the smallest amount of harm. It is something that we have to persist through, this invective to the stars. There can only be the smallest margin, the smallest margin to carry us there.

Listen to the wind, it has a charm to chime the very buffets of nature. And here, where the light comes again and again, there will be a noise so bright that the heaven's themselves will weep white tears, and come back for nothing else.

Verlaine – a weathering that leaves no mast. A sense we all have that the rain will not last. What is now, is forever. What was then, has passed. What the limerick does not take note of, is not important. And then, when last straws are drawn...

Catching the radiance of it all. Seeing, so as to get our fill. And then, when the light of life catches in, there is nothing that stops the irascible bull, nothing that stops its forward motion. And in that motion is life itself. Life itself. Life itself.

Verlaine – Catching the golden thread. Catching all of us in times of difficulty. There is nothing more to see here, except for the circle of hill stops that guide the way. Be a partition in a land of common good. Be that man, and yours will be shouldered.

Grains of sand in a sand dune, measured six foot high. Three is here, more than the delicacy of friendship can pertain towards. This is what you have left, so let us use it with verisimilitude, and then adumbrate the weather. Look here, and see.

Verlaine – And here we are then. Never before have the sights been so visible. Never before have the nuances of care been so lascivious. There is a line in the sand, just here, that does all it can to be, and be stronger than the next.

Gaining in speed, the carriage motions forwards, and gives a sign to the gathering crowd. There is never more that a new dimension to be held in turn of rectilinear direction. And then, a new sense of old thoughts. We will make it. We will.

Verlaine – coming sideways, the rain knows how to swim, and have credit where it is some-times due. There is now a new type of daring that does not hide in reams.

Sitting without a need, and no sense to prevail. There is here, more than levity can share. And when we have seen enough, words come from all places, and in all sets of shapes. The dis-tance does not matter here, only the time we have left.

PAUL VERLAINE

Verlaine – are you the one to fall on missing feet, before the tall sign is erected? Do you never see what is bristled past, and then in a bout of rage, come and tell us what is what? There is more to tell of than a cat's eye, and to bespoke than the rest.

Conformity to the signet ring, is all that we should have. The rest is with the past, and all she has been shown to give. And now, without the simplicity of care, there comes a patch of dan-delions, that in being kept, are kept to treasure. Be there.

Verlaine - Are you drunk again? – He never wrote a bad line – He was weak in all things, ex-cept poetic creation. And that is the price you pay for greatness. And then, when there are no more tears, a restful state descends from some unruly place.

Clinching the next step. There is nothing to say here, except, go! And then when the tigers are fed and watered, there comes a mission on the next horizon, to call the mist its namesake, and listen once more to the time it takes to herd a shallow pond.

Verlaine – Only listen to what the sand says. Only be in touch with the magic of the night. Only be the one to wriggle free from danger one more time. There is a chance here, to climb the highest mountain. We will see it through.

The density of the labour, is nothing other than a force of nature, that has as its compass the boon of a dying breed. And here, where the moisture is not heard, there is a time to welcome in all strangers - all strangers, welcomed in.

Verlaine – the fear we have that time is not enough, will follow us to the grave if we are not careful. And here, where the belief in things is foremost in our minds, there is a saying that is best left unsaid – how do we feel, at the trapdoor and the rabbit.

Gaining in strategic advantage, there is a thing that can, if it is willed, bring down our ship in a twinkle of a worn out eye. But what is this thing? It is something that has heart, but no soul, inklings of nature, but no respite. There can be only this.

Verlaine – do you speculate on the lives around you? Do you have as a compass the dreams of a thousand poets? Do you land in haste in untold destinations? What is this, this we call home? And now, a short reprieve, and then onwards.

Gaining in care that has no flight – simplicity that has only leisure - a burden that has only it-self. There is more than enough time to sense the feeling we have, and to make it real. On the surface it appears opaque, but from within!

Verlaine – majestical, and sincere. The time we have is short, but what is this before us? It is the fire of life. Meant to spray us with hot embers, until all we can do is clean them of, and march beyond! There is never enough to see. Only enough to try.

Bringing in the vestiges of the night. There is a sound, but of what shape? A sense, but of what ilk? A necessity, but of what dimension? There can only be these things.

Verlaine – The night time is with us. And here, where the light only covers what is needed, there will be a chance to see things through. And then, when the night becomes even more receptive, there will shine a cornerstone to bend with.

And now, there comes a crashing sound, that has as its beacon the semblance of things. Do not wander here, this is not the time for play acting. We have the sound of the daylight as she wanders through shadowed places. There is a light, let us use it.

Verlaine – there is not the tempest in oily guise, but the wind in nearby places. The things we have heard of are enough to fill a large bucket with the happening of this to that, forward to back. We must not escape – to escape is to miss the beat.

Hanging on to the shudder of the misanthrope like the windows of a large accompanying ruse. There is now no place with which to sense the other regions of time, as they diminish in stature, and have the sounding board of the many, the one.

Verlaine – come and have a go, there is no place like this to wander and see the occasional desire. What we thought was a misnomer, is nothing more than the levity of an all-out farce that has the might to do what is needed.

There are winters that do not reap. The are canyons that have no depth. In us, there is sim-plicity. In us there is the time it takes. In us there is a plentiful abundance of soul, waiting to be plucked. In us there is everything.

Verlaine – have the half plodding steps come your way? Come your way to Eden? Is this what we have fought for? To be belligerent, in sea-faring mould? To be want of the sands, the sands that keep us back? This much we must hope for.

There are things that must not be. There are curves on blind silk that do not epitomise. There are grains of sand that must only be – and in being, placate, placate the wind through the trees, and then back again, right to the embers.

Verlaine – what is it that the sun has given to you? What is it that the inklings of the stars have never foretold? What have the necessities only hinted at, before it is too late? There can never be a time like this, ever. Never a time like this!

Catching on the seams of the dreaming state, we must not hold folly in the sort of things we wish for. We must not believe in this so solemnly, that from one disaster to the next, is all we see. There must be a sort of mocking at the door, and then – shut!

Verlaine – happenstance and wanting next. There is now a solemn rite, that gives rise to all the ancient bells, as they come raining in twos and threes. There is now a sound for the utmost and terrifyingly low decadent release. We will come.

There are wanderings that have as their direction all the states of Dis. And there, where the moisture runs high, there is a claim to the mantle of all out hardest, that has no sheen nor fathomable want. There is more in spirit than casts a pall.

Verlaine – have you seen the way forward? Have you seen the way to go? It is like a newly found watering shed, that has sprung an unholy leak.

Forests that have no weapon. Describing the sea, and all she is. Being without care, but with sense. The thing we thought was most at ease, and the thing we thought would always follow, has never been so forthcoming as this. Give the light a wink.

PAUL VERLAINE

Verlaine – have you seen the way forward? Do you know which way to turn now? There is something like a new found piece of land, that has not the sequined about it. There is some-thing lasting here, and something to gather the trees – Yes.

The base of the building has on it, a plaque. On this plaque, lies the mystery of history, the history of this place, of this town. And once you have read this plaque, your life is so invigorated, that the tempest cannot blow you over anymore.

Verlaine – there are no more weeds for us to conquer. There are no more things that will say nay. There are only the fathoms that have the recent timing as their grove. The density of waves here leaves us a little perplexed. We will come.

Come and see the race for what it is. Come and see the dance for the dancer's sake. There is not combined yearning here. No scissor step to guide the unwary. And here, where the bois-terous and the morning light have their say, a chasm to traverse.

Verlaine – all the more reason to hear the falconite as she roars into some semblance of the character of life. There is a yawning, and a being still. There is something to light the way for-ward, and then curtail the distance we see.

Having a way through, and all that will pass. Seeing the semi-impression of the lark, and then knowing it to be true. There is never enough to sense the light will still come. Having a fallen mass, and believing once again in fate. There will be time.

Verlaine – do you hamper the stone's throw? Is yours an open window, that hides as it suc-cumbs? Can we see ourselves again in new found wonder, forever nearing enclaves. There is now a sea with briny waves, that have come to save as heal.

A listening that the heart does in times of need. A feeling we all have when we have reached our limit. There can only be this, and this only. There cannot be otherwise, so let the hand's span span, and let the rough edges blur. Never before...

Verlaine – there are nuances to fate, nuances we must not forget. And when our journey is through, next to us lies the harbour and the sea. It is a marvellous thing, this world, a marvel-lous thing, that has no explaining, nor repartee!

Never before have we seen this, or anything like it. There is no time to explain, or give gifts. There is only the gathering, and something more besides. We cannot follow where we want to go, nor climb in amongst the ruins. Be still.

Verlaine – holding on tight we look at the way things are, and are perplexed. Why this, when this is enough to make us dance a new dance? Why not the lessons of a yonder shore? Why not the feeling of a continuation of things?

The half-light catches on the mantle, and evolves into something living. And here, where we have been a thousand times before, there is finally life.

Verlaine – there was once a seeming mist, that had as its toil the verity of the sustained moon. And here, where the gods lie about, in graduating pose, there comes a panel of static that re-leases as it hums, and burns. There will be more...

PAUL VERLAINE

Coming to our senses now, there is a newly found cistern, that believes in nothing else. We will have to curse ourselves, before the harvest gives its relinquishing gesture. Be that as it may, there is never a fledging moment to see again.

Verlaine - are you there? Are you the one to see with new sight? Does the junket and the trumpet make no noise when seen. Does this mode of delivery cause no tension in the ranks of Jupiter, nor in its moon-song. We will come.

There can be nothing to edge in the quiet, nothing to be the one to see, see from afar. There are things we must do, and things we must not do. But these things blur into a spasmodic slumber that has only tears to rub by, and senses to turn.

Verlaine – are we there? Do we stop the show, and start rejoicing? I think so. And then, when the mouse and the bull have had a say on so much, there is now a levity that guides, and an insouciance that holds. Never has the tempest been so sure.

The guiding mechanism is there, but what of the stakes at heart, the things that bind, the courtship that moved beyond. What has the axe to say to the wood, that can rival the sense that the mist has, that things will right themselves, and never look back.

Verlaine – a half sized monument, one that does not choose to honour the dawn. There is now a place for it, in the half-chalice, that winds, and moves in time to the gesture that harks so much. Be in the tangle with us, there is fun to be had.

Gesticulating and proving our worth. Never ferrying forth, without the accoutrements. What has, also has not. There can only be care in the swing of it – in the motion of this turn, to the next. Having the fun to be like a stranger in a strange land.

Verlaine – What have we said, that has never been said? What has been in the right of things, since the very beginning? There is a choice we had, long ago. A choice that came, with numbers and letters. Do we saddle up to the world, and sing?

Gun shy, and rearing to be fathomed. Do not box me in. There is weather in amongst the sta-sis. Do not push in the key, the joy that emerges will knock you over. And here, then a calm in amongst it. Something to savour, before we continue.

Verlaine – a new sense. A new sense of old clocks. What is there to do now, except roll with the punches. I have heard it said, 'you just need to get up one more time than you get knocked over'. And here is a truth. One to savour.

The blessing and the curse. The seeming intransigence of it all. The might and the speed, the dumbbell and the night sky. Where are we now? All I can do is write. And then, when the grindstone is like a character in a book, here we will come.

Verlaine – the carrier pigeon is like the dice from the Nile. Never before seen, and loved to the point of nullity, there are sands here that have no time to bend.

There are wings that do not miss. There are times that do not hiss. And when we are through, a ballast shaft that will handle all the accoutrements. Never before seen, and alongside the best of them, there comes a time for a race. Yes.

Verlaine – I never saw you when you lived, although I was there. It is strange how the past keeps a hold on us. It is strange how the past, while never really there, lays claim to so much. There is never a victim here, never one to play the part.

Holding on for life. Never letting go. Being the one to be sensible, and through it all. Never feeling, always being, always that left cleft of undulating momentum. And here, where the sand does not shift, there will more than a fair share of life.

Verlaine – always opening up, always proceeding with dignity, there are things we must not despise – for to despise them leads to the very shrine we shouldn't be at. There are listenings that toil no harbour, and no sense to give.

Gaining in the surge, there is a warm respite from the gale of our lives, as we twist and turn through the might that is existence, and know our ushered lives to be what we never thought. And what we never thought, is this…a clash of hearts.

Verlaine – What ushers us sideways is not that roaming mass, the mass that has a label on everything known. But now, when we seek the further land, we have found where to sit, and know it to be a place that is urbane, and not in need of sustenance.

Watching as if something was going to happen. Watching as the dawn breaks on silent hills. Watching as the burgundy of the rain falls in a noisy unison. There is never something grander than this. There is sometimes a smooth texture, to be sure.

And then, when the noise does not bark, and the sentience of the night squiggles closer, there is a tempest that knows only light, and sound, and the being of all things. Come now for the rain. Come now for the chance to change things.

Verlaine – there is no opinion, but of the best. There is no charm, but of the worst. There is the way we should be, and the way forward. Never before swimming in comfort brush. There is an inkling to decide on the way. And then, yes…

Gathering ourselves for one last time. Gathering ourselves for the tenacity that is here to fol-low. What we need when need is at its lowest ebb. The following of fireflies through the night is enough to bring down a renegade might. So, there you go.

Verlaine – have you never known a moments rest? Have you wandered though dale and sail? Have you sought the difference in speed for the blackening of light? This much is sure, we will fight the fight of the daring, and soon be here for the want.

Catching something for the rain. Catching something for the water of a mighty sea. Catching something for all that is, and then, when we are through, we place our catchings aside, and let them breathe again. And only then, can we live.

Verlaine – a nice harbour, one that relaxes the mind, heart and soul. And then, when the listening we do is at its height, there will come a more dulcet song.

Insightful to the last. Harrowing to be seen. What there is, is
now what there was. What there was, is now what there is.
And here, where soothing silence reigns, there will be a new
kind of desire. A need for something of the way of things.

Verlaine – a tail spin to launch the new journal! What do you
say, one of promise? We will have our fill of kinds unknown.
And there, in the well-spring, a sense like we never were,
and only have what we thought we couldn't have.

There sits here a time, a time that harbours no fear, yet
remonstrates to the buckle of the cho-sen few. And here, we
start our adventure, and know it to be a blessed thing, there
will be things never to be annulled, and things, well,
somethings…

Verlaine – often times you sit, sit in the café, drinking your
fill, and then what happens – you get up and leave. There is
nothing of the remonstration here, nor the gold lion in the
juvenile sense. There can only be the wanting of the night.

What has happened to the daylight? What has happened to
the night? What can be lost, can never be found. What we
can hold onto, but all that is enough. What is in the air, can
never escape. What is of the moon, is a complement to the
horizon.

Verlaine – are things at rest? Are things at their best? Is this
the way things will transpire now, through hill-up and dale,
through vice-regal prevail, through the ambient tension of a
night time bliss? Come with us, dear one, do not stay.

Ambient, and divided. Seeing what lasts, and what is in the
lead. Seeing the cast and not wanting anything. There is
never a place here, that does not languish. There is never a

place that has a heart of steel. And now, when we are there, forever.

Verlaine – are you the one to take risks? Do you throw the dice, with never say care? Is this the way to go, through the mire, and through the night? There is never a hunting share, in the time of desire and phantom want. Be careful, it is all we can do.

Everything we have wanted is right here. Everything we need, is right here. All we must do is look, and lo, it is found. But that does not stop us in the willing saga. Each placed assemblage never wavers, and never succumbs, only to the breeze.

Verlaine – everything is different, everything is the same. I am bringing a wooden raft for us, so that we can travel to places unknown! Places unseen, places bereft of the settlement of deeds. And when we come for a further look, there is nothing left.

Contagion, and the dire in all of us. There is withheld in this heart more than a moments rest. Come to see things clearer, and what you will find will be, not the naysay, but the winding of winter glass. And here, a might that has all.

Verlaine – what is this thing we divide upon ourselves? Is it the taken and the aplomb? There is a missing beating – but no, we have found ourselves anew. Found the wanting and the surge. We are free, but is this the freedom we seek? Of course.

Gushing, and moving. Be attuned to the centrepiece of life. And when we have more of chance than the wind, there asks a new question, one we can rely on.

PAUL VERLAINE

Verlaine – away, and through, and coming back. What do you say, that has only the mist as a daughter? We have long thought the grains of sand that guide us are here for good. But what of the shards of April, that need new picking. Yes.

Forests and mantle pieces. What is lost, can never be found. What is charged is alight. What is here, can never be seen. What we find when we languish, is the bliss of the moon, as she turns an aqua colour, and whose face is nothing other…

Verlaine – Come and see, see the vast expanse, as she widens the space between us. Come forth, and see the sigh, emitted by the tender and the rush. And now, a blatant arrival, that has as its sense, all the sheaves and rustles of day.

Breaking fast, and seeing the whole world. Be the tendrils of the land that creeps in known motion, and in the end, life will be yours, in a most spectacular means. Be the tension, to see in the new things of the year, and then come and see what is next!

Verlaine – a hopeful start, and then the newness comes. But then, what is that? Something more to say, that is it. But what of the holding, as she comes in fixed need? There is something we must say here too, and that can never be enough.

We are not overreaching, not in the slightest. And here, oh here, there is temporality in the making, stirs of cold wintress, a great layering of things. Do we sit and wait for the call – no, we go forth, until things are mended! And then?

Verlaine – are you fit to leave? Have you the finger on the off guard? Does the rainbow sleep in your honour? Are there more things here than the garden could want? In this, we say, hoo-ray, and then, in a frightful sort of way – 'yes'!

Ranching on the bellows, we sit, and know the time to come is wistful. We hurry ourselves, to make the meeting last, but it is only here I excel. And when the darkness has the light, there will come a time for reason, and a show.

Verlaine – there is now no more to do. No more to say – except this one thing, that cannot be salvaged from any ship, in any point of wreck. See the graveyard of souls unending, as the flash and murmur through the distance. We will be, and be through.

And again – what is left? What is not taken by the vociferous? We can hear the noise of grolnick as it winds away. Do not sense our being, we are here to be enlivened, and then de-rided. We feel ourselves anew, and know that we can always be fettered.

Verlaine – can you bespeak ancient wonders? Can you dream of ancient lands? Is this the way of the vociferous? A never ending pride. What do we say when things are here for the lasting. There is now a time for song, and a time for rejoicing.

Going through the trees as if there wasn't time enough. Having the linen at ease, and knowing where to go to get more. There is a future circus to be played at this site, we should gather, and be placated, and know that the wind is in the making!

Verlaine – have you given everything in your powers to make it work? Have you sampled of the test to see what it is about? Be a marvel, it is true.

PAUL VERLAINE

Grabbing the name sake, and seeing it through. Having a chance to leave the farmlands, and making it work. There is never any love to feel here, only the whispers of regret that carpet the hosing remonstrance.

Verlaine, a new hoard to lauder by. And then, when the moisture rises to the top, there will be a systematic upheaval in the weave of things. Do not drop the bottle my good man, there is a soaking to be had. And here, where we sit again, aplomb.

Nice to be the rupture in the way of things. Nice, simply, to be. There are times in amongst it that show no heart. We may suffer, but our suffering belies no fate. There is often more to be said at these times. But what do we say, when things are full.

Verlaine – the noise of the pasture, does it seduce you? Is this where we should land, in amongst it? Is this where the shards of it lay? In the back of reason, there lies a trick. In it is the trick of the night. And what trick is this? We shall see.

Foraging around a hill that has just seen first light. And here a bone that has never known rest. Never seen the ties that bind us to things unsaid. Never seen the rubber stamp of the valley strewn with love and thickets. We will laugh.

Verlaine – what have you said to the chains that bind? What have you given to the aches that unwind, the teeth that bare, and the willows that slide? We are here, my old man, and that is to say, we are all here waiting for your last oration.

There are feelings we have, that die on no fruit. There are windows that look unto vistas un-known. There are desires that only harp, and then, do not give in. There are mistakes that have been made, that allow only for solutions. We will be content.

Verlaine – what is more, is that in the house of substance, there reigns a nightly curfew. One that does not have the taste of things unheard. We will not perish in the straights of the few, and then, when we are through, a nightly dance.

Gaining in strength, we whistle past the ghost house in the mirror of things, and know our time to be short. What is there now, but the most insurgent daydream that could ever be imagined. We have not envisaged more. And then an encore!

Verlaine, seeping through, not believing the refrain! Not seeing things for what they are, and never finishing last. What is there left, but the handsome drive of a camel on our backs. The listless adventure is here now, without the need to carry.

A greater silence one has never heard! A greater need to see the dawn, one has not seen. And then, with painful slowness, there is the rasp, that has only the foot of everybody's need. Come for the pleasure, stay for the name sake.

Verlaine – can we forgive each other? I think we can. And then, without recourse to the naming of a wonder, there is more than treasures can be. And then, without a new stretch in darkened sand, something we must be capable of, and through.

Thinking of the great chasm that lies between you and I, I know that the sharpness of the bel-ligerent minds will knock the sands from our feet. Yes, and then...

PAUL VERLAINE

Verlaine – are you here? Do you descend from on high? Is this the way we proceed? Down dusty roads, and open byways. There is now here, a sort of fathoming desire to see the way forward, and see it up close, so that we never forget it!

And now, a standing ovation! With this, my Verlaine, you have made the necessary inroads to be completely at ease with life and sequenced with more of what is best. There hurries on us a narrow stream, that lingers in the motion of all that is.

Verlaine – do you seek what cannot be sought? Do you wonder in a dreaming time – a time that is for keeping and not for wasting? Do you see the pinions from on high and know that they are for you? All this is mesmerising, we should follow!

Casting ourselves in bronze, we love the middle of it, and the outside as well. What is there for, but the vexatious, and the quizzical? And then when tender hearts are made to feel free, there will be a life born amongst sombre plains.

Verlaine – a feeling we once had, but have now forgotten (it has been so long!) The tempest cannot let an unruly band of gentries go in solidarity. This much is clear. We have the way, to be solemn, and to be in lurch. Come and be the stuff of legends.

Gaining in strength, the withholding of the feather from above our head bares sweet embrace. And then, the need we have to see victory for what it is, is the way we all see things, all of the time. There can never be anything more than this.

Verlaine – my Verlaine, what have we come to! What have we seen, but things that are un-seen! What are we here for, but the mist? What have we never seen beckon? There are things here that defy explanation! There are longitudes amongst latitudes.

And yes, to see further than we ever have before. This is our goal, and our never seen right. And then when the posture of the king is at issue, we will write a new book, one that is illumi-nated by the sons of Spanish princes. And then, something...

Verlaine – do we counter the strike at our souls, with more of the same as we have been giv-ing? And that is nothing but the thinking of mortal men in times of distress. This is what we thought we always had, a looking into the secrets found astray.

Again, there is nothing, there is only the sands of the hourglass to bind a temperance to the mast. And here where the juxtaposition of this to that, has found no further instrument of de-cay, there is a new sense, that we must unravel by ourselves.

Verlaine – a half beauty in the shores of forgiveness. A new sort of thing that has no recourse to the old. I am used to this now, the giving of half-labels, and the merriment of the long in fashion bores. There can only be what will come.

Come inside for a refreshment, before the tide comes crashing in. Come inside for the cool-ness of the air to subside. I love what we have here, but sometimes this is not enough. That is okay, we will only have a small distance to go.

PAUL VERLAINE

Verlaine – the utmost traipsing over common land, the sense of the wellness of things. And here, what is left, is nothing – nothing but a restive respite!

When things are near, they are not far. When the Trojan call is near at hand, there resides a new heart to be. And when the silence follows there is no perchance to dream. All we must do is call the dream a science, and have our hand at that.

Verlaine - are you here to torture us? In the outward bounds, you are. And here, where the slaying of snow has its temperance over the ice, the bands will come. But they will come, but not as we expect. There is a catching on the water of things.

Giving voice to a hard multiple, that goes on in repetition of itself over hills, and through a curtailing wind. A shipwright, and all that is wrong. What we need is something more besides. What we need is the fathoming to tell us, how deep.

Verlaine – have you seen the gathering for the dust? Have you seen all things in case of need? Have you tethered yourself to the causeway, and never knowing, leap! There are trains that have no glistening stairs. And here, a blending.

What is it we seek? What is it, we have to know? We have to know, what time it is. What time in utter shades. Have we recuperated, so as we can see our calling for what it is. A run-a-away ride that does not shirk the lime-press or the squall.

Verlaine – have a heart, do not be dismissive here. The only way forward is through. The only way back, there is no way back. The only way forward is through. That much we can say. And when we have said it – onwards and throughwards.

The feeling that we thought we would never lose. The compunction to do things in order and in form. Do not belittle the stranger, he is of his own dimension. And here, where we gather for sombre reflection, a note of camaraderie, that holds sway.

Verlaine – are you reckless? Do you feel the calm? Is this where you feel at home? There are things here that have as their sway and swagger the might and steel of a thousand windswept nights. Do not gather in abandon, the timing is just off centre.

And then, without a thought, nor care, there remains a situated appraisal that gives back to the daylight what the twilight has taken. And here finding ourselves not yet astray, there is a sort of bounding temperance that leads to no chase. Forever there.

Verlaine – Hoping and sensing, the forward motion is enough to cut. But what cuts deeper, is the manicure of the soul, that heeds in rushes and in measures. There is now no time to see what is left. What is left are the things that hurry no appeal.

A wishing that has the power of one. Constant lagging that betides the scene. Do not wish for more, there will be a consequence, and a righting of lost shores. And when we are done, there exists a placard to say, yes we are one. Do not vanish here.

Verlaine – a quarter of the time we live is spent simply breathing, and then the rest of the time working/playing/sleeping/eating. And here where the night is in its phase, there is recognition to come, and demi-gods, and utmost song. Find a way, we must.

Taking a hand to seal the vestibules, there are chances at six, to right the ship. Do not hang there, until the end of things. Only be careful with the completeness of it.

Verlaine – have you seen the latest development? – Argh, you are the latest development. And when we sing, we sing for no one else. All hail the great one who transmuted the fire, and had gold instead of rain. Do we love one or the other?

And there, watching the throw of the sand as it beaches on new shores. There is love in this town, love which rides on high. And when the movement of the sea is at an end, we will con-tinue on to the vast plains that await, and know ourselves there.

Verlaine – oh well-wisher, I find the trail that runs through this mountain is like a fathoming we never had heard of. And there in the throes of the accoutrement there sings a fatal lullaby, that has for no man the science of it. There will be more.

The distance from this to that is more than we could have hoped. And then, when the starling writes her name across the sand, there will be a new dance that has not the need to be in the shallows. And then a beauty that outshines all. Yes, a beauty.

Verlaine – a tether that we still need to hold on to. A nuance that tells a wretched tale. And then, when we are through, there will come a rejoicing, that has no fear, and nothing to favour. Tend to your garden, oh trainer of wolves. It will suffice.

Coasting in the way of it. The way of things that has no sharpness, only the sharpness of quill on paper. What is there here to say? What is there here to do? We have never before seen this phenomena, that much is sure. What is left?

Verlaine – what is this thing they call love? You must know, you experienced it on a number of occasions. Is it the township, or the townsfolk? Is it the wanderer in the night, or the gentle prodding of the daylight? We must see all if we are to continue.

Just to trade places with a number of rites of passage. And here, there is a mountain of sticks drawn out in silent wonder, drawn out in the magnificence of it all, to see once again that life is not for strangers, only for the initiators of solemnity.

Verlaine – the tide is set. The rungs are nearest their height. The sturdiness of the valves gives a shine to the window sills. And now, without a missing beat, there coaches a new sense of what to expect. New hills, new vistas, new places to be.

Having said all of that, there is a piece of the puzzle still to be solved. And that is the noise that raindrops make on a tin roof! What can we say to that, and that alone. There is always a chance to achieve the stepping stone. And then, away…

Verlaine – catching a hollowed out barge to our destination. There are barbs here, barbs for the weary. Barbs for the love and abandon. And now, without further introduction, a new way to be! It is like the sand that never was. Shall we?

Holding on tight, tight to the twinkle in the eye, the never evoked standing on rushes in dreaming silk. There can now be no more of the frivolity, now is time for the serious, and the crescendo. I will descend now, to finish what I have begun.

Verlaine – Coaching in lines of rectitude and remiss. The dandelions that perch on the sill have all the strength of the day, and everything of the trailing mass.

Vigorous, and un-blinded. A tutelage in the making. And here, as everywhere, a sense of things to come. We do not listen, you and I. We only acquiesce to the dreaming state. And there, like fire in need of dry wood, a place for the ages.

Verlaine – ah ha. Listening in the woods. Having them come full circle, and being like life itself. There is never a wondering moment in-between. Never a scar written on parchment. The scars of life, poor life. And now a new turn, one that envisages!

Nearing the sense we thought had departed, we try again for all that will be. And there, in the shadows, there it stands, in triumphant attire, and most regal aplomb. And without the desire to sit on sands of radiating sureness, we dream on.

Verlaine – a possibility has awoken, one that say yes, we can do this. Yes we can scurry to where we want to go, and see our life's petals flower. Do you spend your days in idle wonder? Is that the purpose of it all? Is that where we should go?

Forcing ourselves through the pinions of the night, and having a riding fairy barred from entry, there is never more than a moment like this. We stand here, and float as demons on the vine. We will enter, only because we can. And there, did you see it!

Verlaine – all the more decent of you to say, polishing
lovingly the armour of your forebears, now yours – it has
seen many campaigns, and many turns of phrase. And now,
with as much as a thought, the icing on the cake – yes, here
it is! And away!

Forever bleeding, forever found. What is most at risk, is not
the tell-tale being of fortune at waste, but of the languishing
of firebrands that have no eek to mention. There is more
than moisture here, my friends. More than sound.

Verlaine – what is the musk that pertains to this sound?
What is the watershed that has a price above her noise?
What do we say, when things are enough, and the bandicoot
and the zebra have no more lines to draw. Be spectacular in
your being!

And now, without the slightest thought, or compunction, a
night that sees us through to the dawn of things. The dawn
of the estuary. The dawn of the bugle call, the dawn of all
that is, and then some. There is more of a sound than here.
Be commiserate.

Verlaine – do you languish in brief despair, on the shards of
the hour glass? Is this where we go now, floundering on the
missive of our lives? There is here nothing else of
importance. Have a hold on the breaches, their lag is sure
enough.

And now, about the sport. What do we sometimes feel, when
feeling is not enough? Does the sea bring longing, longing
for the cup, and all she bears? There is never more to
transpire than this. But where do we go, I hear you say?
Onwards.

PAUL VERLAINE

Verlaine – let us moisten those lips. Let us believe once again in the sanctity of things. Let us feel no more against time, but for her. Do not languish in chosen company, they are the life-blood of great art. And this is what we must ask for.

The tender-hooks of the rag-time wasting. Be a merry fool, and the signs of life will treasure your domain. Where is that? It is here. Where is that? In the realm above.

Verlaine – heart to heart, and then what comes next. Do we feel the dressing of old wounds? I have a belief in the right of things. There is more than the noise of a thousand reminiscences. And then, without the smidgen of the deserted, the now.

Come and see us dressed in our best. Come and see the wandering of far away places. Do not stand to the echo of things, only forage for the night as she comes to all those who sleep. And when we are through, a moisture that envelops. Yes!

Verlaine – have you sensed the mighty, the mighty and the repetition? Do not have your hands at the side of this place. There is an act to play, so do not be complacent. And here, a liking for the sand. We can make it you and I.

Guiding, and never fumbling. A stitch in the weave of it. A sense we will never really fast. And then, without care nor want, a gate opens, and here, there is the greatest zeal that ever was to be forsaken. Give us the thoroughly ancient.

Verlaine – what has the sandpiper believed in, but all, like us? What have we seen but the silence as it stands. Do not send your ships down this channel, there is more to do. And then, in the afternoon, something to sooth weary limbs.

The chatterbox, and the repartee! Come for the sort of gumption there is here. Come for the notion that things can improve. Come for something else that is not in the way of things. Stand to attention, you are wanted.

Verlaine – there are things that have no sound. There are trees that do not wave in the wind. There are promises that do not diminish. In this we have life. In this we have the soul of things. In this there is hope. Do not scar yourself needlessly.

The father of time itself. The like-minded disciple who rings true of the sand. Do what you will, but do not do this. Do what counts. Do what the waves of an ancient sea could never do. Do what we had always wished. And then, with help, there is sound.

Verlaine – do you sense what it is that keeps us burning? Burning from the top to the bottom? There is a likeminded feeling in the stream of it. And now, when the tops of the trees are found again, something to wait upon, and then never give in.

Having the golden egg, and then treating yourself to a mirror, laden with fruit. I am now a measure in the window of acceptances. Will you come with me? Will you come with the chance to blow a breeze in all directions? Yes, then the turning point.

Verlaine – the snow melts quite easily here. And the sun raises high in the sky. Do not see the road for what it is. The cobblestones will never get in the way. And now with gentle camaraderie, the sounds of the ocean bleed against ancient rock.

And then, without respite – without the need to find the gully again, there is a tempest that harks only trees, and bitter scorn. We have found a way, amongst the embers of existence, through to the acorn of life. There is more here than expected.

Verlaine – feasting from a table that has never known rest. Feasting from a vine that gives life as it takes. Carrying the hurdle with you as you go. Never before seen!

Always sensing what is next – always being the hope, and not the victor. Being treasures un-told, having no hold for the furious. We must run, and in running, be that thing which always believes in this or that. What is this for, anyway?

Verlaine – a novel approach, one that could be the play and the harp. And now, when we wit-ness the storm from afar, we can see what makes it up, and all of it smitten. Do not tell the ranger where to go next. He will only find a way.

And then, when the blanket of life is surely there, there are times that do not weep the longest, and times that do not weep the shortest. And then, when the fill has been had of the journey, a sudden sound, and then the chance at justice.

Verlaine – offspring of the window vase. Never before seen limping and demoralised farming. And there, in that window, life comes in smatterings of pane, and then, without so much as a care, a final piece of the real, to real in. Come in shards, come.

The moisture that only sees itself. The colouring that has only the square to reside in. Never likened to a fruit. Never once believed in courting anchor. Never, ever, sought to sit on pinions made of mesh and wire. And this is what we say!

Verlaine – There is a time in amongst it that we thought would only be there for the basting, and not for the running. There is like a bliss in all of this, a bliss that comes only once a life-time, but we must not rattle forth, we will only injure ourselves.

A ghastly mishap, that has no consequences. A forward motion that lingers in thin air. What we thought was the ring, was nothing other than a phantom. And here, where a drive in a carriage is as good as a trail through the streets. Yes!

Verlaine – commitment to the journey, the journey of a life-time! Never before heard, and never before seen. Crash and enveloped! Never once seeing which way is up. There can only be one way, and that is through. This much is true.

Closer now, than ever before. We walk through fields of grey, fields of stone. And here where the life of it perplexes, a new random epiphany keeps guard. And like the steel of it could not hanker, the moon and all her ghosts prevail.

Verlaine – all the more true. All the more to believe, and then take on board. All the more wor-ry, to have as a minding guide, and then, to seek out, as the sun has a heat. There is nothing left of you and I. Nothing to cast the embers into, either.

Forests that perch to the very top of the hill. Vexatious, and roundabouts. The listening we have so far done is not for ourselves, but for the combined yearning of the stars. There is a fact here, that cries out for the fence and all that will sit on her.

Verlaine – have you thought of Rimbaud in a little while? Of course you have. Your greatest influence, your greatest disaster. There are things that have as their sail all the putting's of yore. And here, a new type of seed, one that does not bight.

A greenery to overcome. A nest that does not hurry. There are languishing's that have no price. And here, where we once were, never a thing to see.

Verlaine – are you the cost of a thousand nights labour? Have you risen in seats of gold, whites of no compare? In this way, we move forward, and have as our air and graces that which is utmost in our minds. Do be dishevelled here, it will suit.

Gaining against the banister, we rally in fortunate change. And then, when the night-time has as its voice the distant heartbeats of a long and indebted speech, there is now somewhere to go! Don't be a thing to remind us of. Be a thing to impel.

Watching carefully as the sun goes down, we last another heart-beat into the future, and then return for an upgrade of sorts. And then without a care in the world, millimetres and centime-tres. We can try which at our disposal.

Verlaine – having the watch and seeing attitude. Being of that course of action that only puls-es. Giving, and taking – hearing and seeing! Being adjusted to the depths of things. Having that which cannot be in line with the sun. Being true.

A magical place to be, 19th century Paris. Where the poetry was hard, and the difficulties hard-er. But each had their lot, and none were betaken by the stream. And then a harrowing belief, and then gone. Some will stay, while others will go.

Verlaine – matching the shirts of the rapacious, but not ending in the cycle, here we laugh at the start of something to say! And then, when the lights are off, and the colour has returned, there is something new to see, and then, finding our way home.

What there was, and what there now is. What is left, and what can never be. In the mist, a long searched for malaise. One that we welcome with arms wide open. Thinking about the time with friends, that is a sport worthy of the field.

Verlaine – have you succumbed to the tree of life? Have you hoped for more than is possible? What is the muse behind this juncture, this tenable life? There can only be what there is not. There can only be what is in the midst of it. Yes, we will come.

Flashing the fleece around the bends, there is more than we can vanquish. Do you gather on ice made from clay? Is that where we seek, in times of trouble, times of fate? And then, when we are near, and everything else is far, a noise, and then, yes!

Verlaine – verily, and yet still breathing. What the soldier never sees. And then, when the light comes crashing, a little way to go yet. There is always sanctions on the heart. The heart of lead, heart of sand. What's more, the times will unleash!

Gaining that thing called motion – commotion maybe? And then when we see no longer, the eyes will keep going, and the solemn rites of maze will relinquish us. And then, before we are really ready, a sweetness in the movement of things.

Verlaine – what have we to see? What have we to know? What is there to be, but all? There can only be what we see, and here, where the lands are like cinnamon, and to move carries honesty that step further, there will be enough to say, yes!

Carried up that hill, where there are no more things to do, we will find ourselves a new cap, one that does not know its place, nor its time. Be a wonder!

Verlaine – there are taps that do not turn off. There are dandelions that do not know when to stop growing. What we have here are the threads of an all-night throng, that displeases as it commutes. Do as we say, and no person will be there.

And then, with an almighty crash! The noise of the thunder arches through the encampment, and then, with an all out poise, a nonchalant appeasement, one that throws tidings aside, there is life, and all that shall be.

Verlaine – when will you call for us? When will the people dance in sullen uncertainty? When will it all happen again for the unwary? There is never enough to simply be, so why worry? Come and carry us away, under tree, under vale.

Forests that undertake nothing. A sharp rise is the moonlit shadows. What we come for, is not what we say is left. A little bit at a time. What is now in harmony, and what used to be in dis-cord. There are trees amongst us, but they will not hurt us.

Verlaine, a ceiling that knows no limit. A feeling that knows how to dance. And when we laugh that bitter laugh, there is no telling what we might achieve! But here, where the sand through the hour glass measures much, there will be a sense to stay still.

Forever breathing that deeper breath. Forever cold in a warm land, Forever bending up the stairs, and then back down again. What is this we have found, but the sounds of everything. What have we known, but the worn out cloud.

The distance is here. The distance we love to fight. And then, when the raising of the shore comes again, there will be time to jump to that further place that has no tempest, nor no flight. Be the one to salvage, and yours will be applicable.

Verlaine – what is the feeling we once had, but have now forgotten? What suffering is this? How does it eventuate? What means has it at its disposal? There is no tide here. No backward and forward motion. I am right of foot. It will not come.

The veritable lane of acceptances. I come for you, but where do you reside? There is a nestl-ing place below the rocks, that is where I live. But what of the tide, and where does it come from? It comes from a nowhere place, and when we see it, aplomb.

Verlaine – have you sat, where your feet should be? Is this where the chasm departs? There are new senses that never find solace. Never endure more than this. Never in all your life times. But what does it matter – we are safe.

Catching on to something strong. Catching on to the blueprint of everything. There is never more purpose than this. And when we are through, a nesting, that rivals that places we have never been. There is luck in the windings of fate.

Verlaine – an ancient claim. More rectitude than can be found. A little more of the side, and less of the front. Be that person. Be that person who does not give in, and then win.

Forests that have hardship as their dominion. A lamentable fool, who has the last laugh. Can we see what it is that keeps us growing? There will be sense.

Verlaine – do you have half a heart? Is that half full with plenty? I wish to examine your vestige – are you amenable? A vestige for the aeons. A vestige for the silk. And now, something that will convince the wary traveller to once again sing!

Can we be perturbed at nothing? Can we shake hands with the devil, and have it remain bot-tomless? There is something here, something like the pigeon hole of the daylight that moves in tractions and in squeals.

Verlaine - is this a weaving, to and fro? Is the might we find, amenable to the sun? Can we climb in ledgers half felt, and next to no time find that the chalice binds, and the ring of half thought guesses melds into one?

Being in love with the journey! Never before seen desires! What we felt would not cure us, has knocked us flat. And here where the leaves have been blown a thousand miles, there comes a sweetness that sizes in disarray!

Verlaine – what do we say to you, oh one of mysteries? What do we say to one so fit of ages that to carry him would mess the bench with cold water. Snap too, there is a chance at forever. And here, we launch into things with bravado!

Foraging, and wanting less that has ever been the vector in an unknown land. I cannot see things as clearly as you, that is for certain. Be the one to tally, and yours is the end game. Be the sense we have to be like the wind, and we will be faithful.

Verlaine – having more to do than ever. Spent forces rallying under the cry. Being in tune with so much. Being worthy of the sun. Hoping not to transgress – well too much. An evening that can never be forgotten.

Being in the midst of it. Catching on, to take hold. A wealth of knowledge, that never leaves. What we say when we are in need. What we love when we are away. And here, where the solace is deeper still, we will find a way.

Verlaine – deeper still, and yet unmoving. We will find the sand as it moves, and the long lost night as she spills. Deserted and unnerved, there are places we should not go. And then, even despite ourselves, a new hitch to ride the stallions home.

Being gone before hand, being that which does not elate! Having the sound of much, and yet standing still! What is this we have in store? We have the lever and the canker. But what of that which lies next? The semblance of all.

Verlaine – What do we say now? What is there left to say? We are listless on a heaving sea. What trope do we sing for now? It is the hour of our birth. It is the now, so we help, and not hinder. Feel and not repose.

A feeling we once had, but have now translated. The motion of the celestial spheres. What is mixed with the clay and the dirt. What we thought would usher in a new life. What we know to alter things irrevocably.

Verlaine – that which does not stop! That which has as it quarry mountains of dust, mountains of memory. And here, where we sit again, a sense to see things anew.

Hanging on, for the sake of all those who have gone before. And then when the mist vanishes, a sense that the right moment will eventuate, and we will see ourselves once again in times of glee. And, yes, a new way.

Verlaine – the tailspin will not suffice. And here, where the boisterous and the languid feel in mutual harmony, there will be a song that does not deliver, to any one, or anybody. Be the one to dance, and it will work!

Catching the moisture before it hits the ground. Curtailing things that have only might. And there, in the middle of the rainbow, a new colour, one that has never been seen. We will fight for it, until the shards of death are no more.

Verlaine – do you catch the last ferry, the one bound for home? Is this what we expect, to be tossed about like a sea's engine, only to gather pace again, so that we may know the channel for what it is? Come, we will go.

Hiring fishermen to catch only leather boots! What we have here, is something we wish we should never have. And then, when we are free, a release into something with depth. Do you sound the way, man of the sea? Do you sound the way?

Verlaine – marching forward, we sense what could never be sensed. And here, where the round-stone does not block our entrance, we will come in solemn ways, and then, despite the champion of things, we will fashion a new abode.

Onwards, people of the night. Onwards to the great promised land. We have no vested interest in the song of things, so let's us fly, and bedevilled by what we see. Come now, there is nothing to fuss about. There is only this, and this only.

Verlaine – hoping to establish a way of life that does not envisage anything from the sea. Im-possible! I hear you say. Everything is from the sea, in some capacity or other. And here, where we languish, another chance at the fall of the dice.

Coming with bravado, coming with comments from the abyss. I hear your words oh great one, and know you to be a soothsayer. Be the whisper in night, and ours will fill a soul. Come to the being in existence, and there forward through what is next.

Uphold the stance. Uphold the way of things. Be the troubadour if the troubadour won't. And then, when we find a way through, that does not stand on the toes of angels, here, oh here, there will be much fun to be had.

Verlaine – be together in the misnomer, the misnomer of the night. Be the person who will find a way, find a way through nothingness to the beyond. Go and sense your new need, that has as its rake old tidings, and older songs.

What have the fellow guardians to say about the wishing before tea? There are new tasks to perform, and new fathoms to engage in. The sense we have that the diminishing of the fall is not a thing we can be without. Not be here, I will tell you.

Verlaine – be the masthead above the symbol, and what will be next will have its laughter in fields of grey, fields of yellow. We are here now – take rest.

Verging on neverness, the laughter we feel exercises our deeper feelings. And then, before we are really there to say what is next, we have an adjacent crescendo, that buckles in times of strife. Do not belittle us – not yet anyway.

PAUL VERLAINE

Verlaine – have you seen the rain, a thing that reaps as it sews? There is a precipice here, that we cannot climb up to. But before then, lights will shine on beings vast in number. Too vast to actually count on. The lullaby is strong.

Invading lands with sullen silk. There can only be what there is. And when we encounter the stead from below the valley, there is enough in our basket to weave a merry handle. This han-dle, this handle, does not shirk.

Verlaine – do you know where you are? Have you the feeling that the sunlight will not touch! Be in tune with more than you can say, and all that will be left will be hands on touchstone. The vagaries of the method. We will see.

Cosmopolitan, and dreaming of the life to lead. There is more than we can see, so let's see it! There is the smell of old things here. There is a well full of water. There is something stranger than snow. We will listen carefully.

Verlaine – what we saw through the mist, we will not see again. What we saw in the valley, cannot be writ in stone. And then, a marking place, that says so much, about so few. Do not sit here, the ropes are slippery.

The ghosts of tomorrow. The wind beneath the meadows. Something singing where it shouldn't. I have love, but not in measure. I turn the corner, and it turns me. I love the way we dance, but only so often. Catch me now, I will not fall again.

Verlaine – do you see the pests on the table? Just leave them, they will disperse of their own accord. And now, before we are complete, a never before seen scene, between two lovers on the esplanade of decadence, and here, we wait.

A condition of entry – well there are none. Bring yourself, bring others, bring the night sky, or it will bring you! There is dust here, of a thousand years. Thick, absorbent dust. We will gather it, like the whims of ancient sailors, now gone.

Verlaine – does your wisp enter on the breeze? Do you have the fire to light your weary legs? Is this what we do for inspiration? Of course! And then without a further thought, we will away, and be in the course of it.

Draining away the liquid, we see what we never can. And that is the sort of thing that can never diminish a soul. And here, where the vertical meets the horizontal, we will be delighted in utmost rendering. Be the lark, it will suit.

Verlaine – have you read the new edition? Have you seen it down beneath, on wild and wet shores? It is amazing isn't, how the raging sea maintains its beauty in its wrath. Can you name another? Probably!

Caught on rocks of grey, rocks of white. I am hanging here, without the need to spoil the sce-ne. And here where we laugh, we know our sense to be true.

Verlaine, do you come again in silk? Do you ride the waves in treasures to be? I have felt it once before, this gaping mass, and know it to be a tune we can never recount. Be that as it may, we will not stumble, we will only say, 'Hello, how are you?'

Being one to gather up the chains, and sort them again according to rank. There are things here we must decry, but that is okay, as is the whim of all things. There are tensions in the trees, I know their bark. And then, once again, away.

PAUL VERLAINE

Verlaine – a happenstance of yesteryear. We will not fight it
– we will roll with it. And roll we will. Do you say how, how,
and then, wow? That much is written on the eggs of seagulls
as they fly to a higher plateau.

The tenor of it does not please, but we say for our lives,
come, come and visit the park before daybreak. There are
things moving here, and things not leaden of foot. We will
not hear the time – it is out of reach.

Verlaine – do you have the skill to drag down a mountain
top? If you do, then the sands that remain on top will be
yours. I am no longer crying. I am blistering for the motion,
and then, a whimsical tale.

What we have here, is not what one would expect. There is
the whispering of autumnal dreaming to keep us all awake.
We will fight for you my friend, for where you live. And then,
say no more of the willows, they will beckon again.

Verlaine – what is there here, amongst the brambles and
thickets? There is a sense of worth, that has only the stars
upon which to shine? There is never a moments grace here
in amongst it. We will find away, we will know ourselves to
be ready!

Caught in a quasi-landslide, that has more to reckon with
than a yard of salt. And here, where the diluted mixture of
life and soil come to march on solemn ground, there remains
a window to the soul, that only a pioneer could handle.

Verlaine – comes crashing at speed. But what is this, this
that turns the table? I will not shirk nor give in, despite any
error by any known species. But wait, the now approaches!
What shall we glean, but a new state of the aegis?

Immeasurable, and delightful. Measuring in the night. Hoping to come that full circle. Love and laughter. Never before seen glee. And then, a semblance of the night. One that we can never out do. And now, before we are lost – clovers, and respect.

Verlaine – I have known no goals other than these, and that is to be a wonderer in a wandering land, to have known peace, and let it shed. These ornaments are a testament to the spirit of things. And before we know it, surprise!

Reaching for forever, and not having to say so. I once knew happy times, but they are now gone. At least I can say, at one time I was indeed happy – is that possible? – now let's have some fun. Fun to lampoon the web of things.

Verlaine – what do we say now, oh man, oh man of strings? There can always be something for us. There can always be the tempest rolled in sheets.

Casting into the fire, dreaded memories of things undone. But now, with some help, there is the way of things, that we do not dread. And here, where the dominion of stone rises to the top, there will be a fallow time of year.

Verlaine – We approach you in the swing of things. And here, where the base metals are all turned to gold, there is a once and future belief that belittles nothing, and has as its hand the steel of future generations. We will come to play.

The mistress is yours, Verlaine, the mistress is in the way of it. Be the cause of our delight, and what you will find is the masthead of hope. Hope for a better life, hope that things will be as they should.

PAUL VERLAINE

Verlaine – the things that catch, are the same things that have fury at their spine. Do not lan-guish underneath. There is more to life than that. There is more to the trench than depth. We must overwhelm ourselves here, and be free.

The feeling we once had that life was a spoil, and the motion of each being in the sea was a symphony. We are here to weather the storm, and see our buildings erected. We will come again, when the time is right, and the wind a grand southerly.

Verlaine – The testimonial is here, as the sand will have its fill. The ditch is deep, but we are tall. Never fall to pieces here, we only come to pay our respects. And now, before we are gone, a light to guide the way. And something else, to be sure.

A fire that does not last. A weaving in-between things that never leaves. Falling towards the heavens, as they hurtle skywards. Never seeing a way out, but always finding the way home. A sense that we will just make it.

Verlaine – there is something to be said about the difference in sizes between this tree and the next. There is something we do not see, when we look. And then, in repose, and in dampening moisture, there comes a time to shake it all off.

A chance we have to follow the stars, in and out of adventure – in and out of love. And then when the masthead does not fall, we will sit on its strength, and know it to be a thing that will take us there. We will not sit though – we will stand!

Verlaine – coming too close to be sure. Coming from a position that is draped in moonlight. Never before seen.

Never before done. Never, in our wildest dreams. We can see the forest floor in dreams of thickest potential. Dreams.

Foraging for the daylight – there is light in these hills! And then a new harvest, one to send the light barricading in time to the world. But what of this world? Where does it come from, where is it going? There can be no more of the trope.

Verlaine – once, upon sitting down dishevelled, we again rise, and see our fate before us. I never knew the future to be of milk and straw, and the past to be of chaff and liquorice. But what about where we are now? Let us find a way.

A cross in the road. Where do you lead? Where do you come from? Further remonstrating to uncover what it is we seek. And then, something that only shocks.

Verlaine – do you see what we see? Do you counter the yoke with the seed? Is there more to life than you think? Do we see past the foible to carry the chain? An echo – I hear it, do you, my Verlaine? Do we see past each other, now?

Conjuring something of a trick to cool the nerves. What was once a catching of raspberry's in the night time waltzing, is now the time for fledging stirring. We will come to the front, and see our destiny as it calls forth in tunic array.

Verlaine – what is that which you are looking at, my friend? Is it the moisture in your hat, or the time it has taken you to climb these stairs? I would think your next bout of noise will be the one that will still us all. Do not be placated in this world. No.

A vestige to cause a draught. A nuisance to belie the fact. There are kind things which should not be said, as there are cruel things just as poesy. And then, when the night is like a vapour, the tempest will have neither, for here nor there.

Verlaine – a trap door that leads nowhere. A wind chime that has no sound. A cloud in the sky that looks like nothing else. And here, where the wind is like a caged animal, there is a taste of freedom that jumps and bites.

Calling the guards to duty – calling all hands on deck. There is something that lingers in the mist of time itself. When we see ourselves again in causing this arrow to fly to this point. Do not envision a dreamscape more worthy. We will come.

Verlaine - is this the thing that blows, and rains blows upon our weariness? I cannot see the vapour for the life. I do not sit unhinged here anymore. Do you fend off with the last of it? Do we all fend off with the single thought in our minds?

In the inside, a remonstrance, the heeds no warning. And then, when the clouds go that deeper hue of red, a new sense of what can be. There is only what we have found to be true. And in this truth itself, a wondering full of life.

Verlaine – my hands are full. My hands no longer have their strength – only for this, my friend, only for this. I have learnt a valuable lesson today – not to overshadow the wind as she spills from heaven. Yes, this is true.

And then, without even a notion of respite, there comes the energy to continue – once, twice, three times. And then, before we have even known it, a message to send forth – do your best, it will come full circle, and when it does, yes!

Verlaine – are you with what matters? Verlaine, yes you, are you with what matters? There can only be one drive of the carriage left, and then the solstice of life renews. Do we see ourselves resplendent, and in knowing tones?

A catechism in the wind, blowing this way and that. You cannot follow the dreams of average men and women, but what you can do is see them reflected in mirrors made of gold, made of silver, and who can shape them that little higher.

Verlaine – have you seen the daylight once again? Or are you locked away in the midst of carriages at the ball. Love me twice, or thrice, if it suits, but do not save me!

The message is here, those things which bight, are the same that come in the night. I play rhapsody with all the things that make me clear. And then, when the further we go, and the further we are there, the further we act in accordance with things.

Verlaine – are you the one to teach the rules of engagement, Verlaine? Are you the one who always sees the truth, before our very eyes? And then, when the starlight does not nestle, there are rituals we must engage in to appease the nature of things.

There is a justification for each act of volition, and an act of contrition, for each solemn act. And now, when the time is right, a sense that we now have that things will turn out right! Now that we can jump – we jump.

Verlaine – are you the one to see things affected? Are you the one to believe once again in the sanctity of life? There are things we must not do, but things we must. And here, where the wind blows in abandon, there is nothing more to do.

Forever pushing over the ebb of life – forever seeing things anew. I am the one to see things as they are. I am the one to relinquish things that bit further. And then, when the stars are in silence, there is a constant noise that has us at our beck.

Verlaine – I see things as they near. I see the moon as she sheds the light of a generation. There are things here that do not weep, but we weep, soldiers of a better day. We weep, but they have it for themselves.

Gushing with applause, the sentiment she speaks of is alone and with flurry. There resides a puissant nature in every beating heart. There is a sense, a need, to tiptoe through the forest, and know it to be a slater of souls.

Verlaine – do you love what is becoming in all of us? Do you see the final bridge, and see the torrent that lives beneath? There is no longer any other way. The only vestige we have left sings a moral tune, as you know, Verlaine!

Coming into the sea of things, and knowing the absolute heart that gets you through. Being forever lonely, but not minding. Being blind but having the courage to carry on. Are we on the fence of things? – No. Do we see again – yes!

Verlaine – Caught in a sound of wayfarers, as they come once again into the light. I have felt more on this journey than in all my life-times, but that is fine. There can only be one way, and that is up. Up, and indeed, up again.

Caught in tethers made of silk, tethers made of gold leaf. There are things that do not hide, and we feel the time is right to sense the woe begotten out. There are now things which do only creep at night, and we are not amongst them.

Verlaine – wishy, and washy. Having the sense to do things twice. Having the sense to be what we want to be. And now, letting the leaves fall on matted grass, we come full circle, and love where we are led. Sometimes, we ache, ache for home.

Forests in the night, simplicity in hand. There comes again the mystery of acceptances. And then, when we least expect – aplomb, and figuring greatly.

Verlaine – do you pine for well-made silk? Is this where we are the most translucent? Come and forward us another missive. Your feral is enough to hold sway. Never come for those who wait. There is a chance here. We will take it.

Barnacles that shiver to life. Sweet daylight, are you waiting? I have found the solution to life. What makes writing work, makes life work! I now say unto the masses, be at home, at hearth, and the tempest will be gullible enough!

Verlaine – do you speak in untold tongues, in measures that are old and new? Do you hope to have the silence that we all had as children? What is this that keeps us moving? What has the time, also has the spark.

Nestled in sweetly, there is more to say – will you say it my sweet Verlaine? Will you say it as if it never happened? Come to the night parade, there will be adventure and excitement, and intrigue. Do not stop, there is a calling card waiting for you!

PAUL VERLAINE

Verlaine – is this the way we stand? Stand in front of another? There is more to do here, like a quirk in the arrangement. That allows us to see into things, and make things work. To do, is greater than to be. That make is found.

There is life at last, life in the vagaries of time. Do come as you please. There is effort in the meaning of things. But what have we? More than the ancient wisdoms, or their font. Come for the pleasure of it. Just simply come.

Verlaine – what is ever of the gist of it, is not in our veins. There is required a verisimilitude to fairly describe the scene. Never once have we thought in squares. Never once have we thought to be is to be like everything we have known before.

Casting adrift in a strong sea. What we thought was the end of it, is not what, now, we thought at all. The time it takes to bury a hatchet is not the same time it takes to wander through the hills, holding back our alarm.

Verlaine – are you here to take note? Are you here to derive pleasure from the pain of things? There are now new things to do, and new ways to carefully idle through the hours of this fara-way place. Do not stand alone, as we will stand for you.

Are you here to say what you like? Are you here, to be a bench in a landing yard full of grain? Is this what we look for, the measure and the ounce? There was once a magnificent column here, but look how it has changed!

Verlaine – The gregariousness of the journey belies its state. And when we are through, the testament to the belonging is not enough to care for the need we have to knuckle down and have the soothsayer come to bare. Yes, yes we will.

A lantern in the darkness, one that does not shout out! And here, a new type of belief, that ties into the old, and gives the blueprint of life. But what of the skies, that known only blue, and black of night? What is there, lot and thimble?

Verlaine – having a lot to say, and more to savour. What is there to hang on to, other than the vignette of life? Be beseeching, like an arm in a sling. Come what may.

There comes a truth, that does not know its own name. There comes a happenstance, that brings with it an ocelot of good tidings. Bear a steady climb, up through the windpipes of a fur-ther channel. Do not be surprised to find the wind.

Verlaine – are you safe? Do you tie yourself to leather leggings that have no dish to fry. Come for the temptation to pair ourselves with the moon. Come for the new redemption of old claws. Be that which we never could.

Having something new to say! Then let us say it like the unfolding of a waterfall! And now, what we have said is written down, and cast in bronze. We will see what we can do. (And then, an envelope from a teacher).

Verlaine – catching a surprise, catching it in full regalia. There is a new source to our adven-ture, a new way to go forward. And here, where the cold does not bite, there is a sense that we can have that belonging that we once had.

Having a great time, only not seeing the distance for what it is. And when we have not seen the fence for the rival, there is a line to demarcate the new type of web. But what of this? What can we truly make of this?

Verlaine – holding on to strings made of fur, the placatory noise does not diminish the sound. And then, with a new sort of echo, each noise here dissipates through the mist, and has as its compass what we never thought of, until now.

Finding more than is required. Having the staple of the life bend that ever so slightly. Never being one to shirk. Never being one to carry the breeze further than it is willing to go. There is a sea sickness here that comes in halves, and stays in fits.

Verlaine – have you a way to go? A way that will find you arranging things nicely? And then, when the sandstone of the buildings couples against the stairs, there is a symmetry that hardly says a thing. And now, a new chance, one that will bring.

What is it here? What is it here, that trades window sills for souls? What is the length of time that it takes to bend a feather over a new mound, a mound made for the outstretched? There can only be something more, and something less.

Verlaine – the sorts of nibs that carry with them the fibres of the news, and that can decry the nuance in the base. If we had time to let the dandelion slip from our grasp, but then return, and allow us to paint a large canvas.

The further we go on this adventure, the more difficult it becomes. And then, when the trade of fireflies in autumn twilight is at a standstill, there will come a new trade, one of silkworms in a dashing grey. Or perhaps aqua? We will see.

Verlaine – are you one to leave already? Verlaine - We are only over half way! No, that is good. I am glad you will stay. My heart is at rest. The steel in my invectives needs no other person. The gods shine upon me!

A flight of geese – but which way do they fly? Whichever way they want. But which way do they go? Whichever way they desire. That is the truth of it.

Verlaine – feathers in the dead of things. Feathers that are translucent to the sky. There is a vastness that heralds all she says. And then, when the night has clutch of the day, the dawn bespeaks what is next. Hear her story.

Forever feeling young – is this a curse or a blessing? Forever feeling like the times have come. There is a phase we all go through, that says of the tempest, come now, you will not falter. There is much weight to carry here, amongst other things.

Verlaine – is this the way to go? Is this the way we have chosen for ourselves? And for our children? Never before seen. Never before felt. But what of this? What of this travail? Where has it come from? And where will it lead? I will make art of it!

Forests that do not sleep. The sea, the sea, that does not sleep. Where are the sounds of life here? Where are the beating of drums in deepest caves? Where are we now? What have we come to? What is it we fight against?

Verlaine – is this what we have to offer? This thing, that is no thing, that is the pressure, and the bearing, and all that it gives. We will not find ourselves again – or will we? There is a chance we will find what we seek. Yes, tell me.

Multiplicity, and that which tears asunder. There is here, in the mist, a kind of guessing game, a game of which thing comes next. We will not be placated any longer, we must be once again admitted to the palace of yore.

Verlaine – is this what we need? Is this the ground to my knight? Is this the way we sing of the promised land? Catching through to the infinity of things, we meander in a sort of chosen timbre, and then, cannot find our way down. We will find a way.

Ghosts that speak no name. Where are they now? Do they succumb to the nearness to the flame? We must let them through, and let them be seated. They are here for us, here to give a message. What message is this? You will see!

Verlaine – cataclysms come early to us. We are familiar to their ilk. Do not belong here, as I do. There is a sort of mess here, that is like no other. We clean but for what reason? This is where we stand, so do not be perturbed. We will find a way.

Launching ourselves at the problem – it is true, it must always come to this. But what of the feather of dimensions? – what of this? There is a misnomer to be vanquished. There is a light that has no flame – be as it may, we will light the fire, still.

Verlaine – is the test still to come? When I am at my wits end, and can scramble no further. What is this, the plenary cries! There is more than sense, sense to dangle in shirts of gold, shirts of silver. There can only be the test to come.

Gaining in strength – we know where we are going. It is not the destination that concurs its weight, but the calibration of all that gives guile to the chase. There is more to see on this road than ever has been juxtaposed in daring, and in light,

Verlaine – there is a sentience here, beside me, as I swim the Hellespont, and what it says is never to capture the sun. Let us launch into it!

The falcon in the air – what has it become? It flies, but to what avail? And now we see the real purpose of things. Teleology what's more. I have said less in my past. I have only now seen more. We will come at things anew.

Verlaine – are you the one to wander – through shallow lands, and hunter's bliss? There are things we must do here, things we must not waiver, must only hint at, and then do with utmost vigour. There are turns of phrase, but there is truth.

Farcical, and alarmed. We do not assemble here. We only assemble in the love made easy pose that has something of its blemish in the nectar of things. What is there left of us? What can we see that can bring us together?

Verlaine – do you will your way to it - so that you can taste the fruit of it? Such is the banner of the tidings. Such is the goliath of the sand, and what comes next! Do not set a foot wrong in here, it will hurt. There is a mess here to be cleaned.

Forests that have no fruit. A farmhouse that lets no visitors. Storming the barricades like sol-diers in the night. Having something to tell of. Being boisterous in a boisterous land. What we see is never enough. What we feel!

PAUL VERLAINE

Verlaine – you are watching with deepest pleasure, your life is over, but what of your legacy? You are better known in France than rest of the world, held in regard above even Rimbaud. Your trials took you there.

The test is in the water. The test is in what we think of the daylight as it comes raining down from above. There is never a solemn search for the bones that are left to lie. In the meantime, there is silence in the wind, so we are worried.

Verlaine – do you sign your name with a flourish at the end? Do you have the sense to see things aright? Do you know where to look, when looking is difficult? There are traces in the sand of people who are here to vanquish. Is that us?

And afterward, where the noise beckons from afar, we will do it only once, so that things turn out for the best. And now, where the junctions of time and longing meet in abandonment and care, there sees a lane through the houses.

Verlaine – we are trying to do what others could not. Carry a mighty ember through the doors of hell, and then back again. But wait, we have things to be by, and to loosen the chains with. Never fall on beckoned road, without the scene to carry you.

Gaining in momentum, the treasure we have always had is now visible through the trees. And then, when the marked soul belittles what the aforementioned has said, there will be a cusp in the waiting, and the dearest will be sewn.

Verlaine – the surest delight that is given to us on this way, is the sand that has no desire to be, or want to thrive. And here, where we no longer feel, the bygone invective feels its way to the top, and knows solace as a thing to weep by.

A harsh blanket indeed, one that harbours more than the steel of thirty nights. And then, when we are left to wander, there comes a door that hurries us all.

Verlaine – happiness is the way we swing from this point to the next. Happiness is the journey we take to cool our weary boots. And then, when the arch of happenstance reverberates through the lostness of time. Here, oh here!

The throng is upon us. But what of that? There are in this world a thousand things more ardu-ous than that. Never once come into the shade, where, here, there is a solemn shape that bends no leaves, and has no life to travail.

Verlaine – having the chance to breathe once again. Having the chance to be who we want to be. And then, in the midst of it, a crowning of glory that never belittles. Have you seen the distance that is nothing in the middle of it?

Caught in the river, and the silence of the flow is overwhelming. I have time to rectify the sea-sons to the tune of bending. And here where the rooves are slate filled, there is a chance to resound in boisterous abandon. We will come.

Verlaine – the newness of it all astounds. And then, without the slightest care nor delight, there wins a purple colour into the march. Do not say we are free – there is more to come. And now, with backs arched, we come again for the sound of all.

In the most arduous time, there is respite in the dry. Respite to say, yes, I am suffering. Res-pite to say, yes it is okay.

But what do we really feel? What is in us, that is really there.
Noth-ing, and then the rattle bag of love.

Verlaine – have you the honesty to keep going? Have you
the motion of the stars to keep you company? Is there a
rainbow that stops at your feet? There are new tactics in the
swim of it, new ways to send a trench, and burry it deep.

Fine and with exemplary flourish. Fine and with the nous to
be called back. Fine, and then without the need to be
concerned. There are marks on every face, that cry out for
this. Do not let things slip, or move forth in wonderment.

Verlaine – have you caught the train to new destinations?
Have you met Rimbaud at the sta-tion yet? Is there a place
never to be found, at least for a thousand years? What do
we say when we have seen it – 'Ouch, and forever staid'.

A chair we must not sit upon! On this chair there is a life.
The life of someone who does only turn for the right reasons.
And then without consciousness found, there is a half
gesture that does not stay still. What is this? We are wont to
know.

Verlaine – what say you, have you a vault? There is nothing
like the starry night to blend chances with the sky. And then,
without a quickness in our step, there is more than the last of
it. Come and gather for the sounding, a board to the quick.

Glaciers, and deemed persons, what is there we cannot
see? What is there we cannot be? What is there, anon.
What is there, beyond? And then, despite the heavy
distance, there comes a crying in the sense of it all. What
can it be?

Verlaine – off to carry the wood. Off to treasure a new barn. Off to wander up right to the mo-tion of the maybe's. And then, without respite, a fallow plot.

Mischief in the middle of things. Delight in the pasture. There is never a reason to give in. There is never a sign from the book that we can't stay. There is a place amongst it all, that harbours what we do, and tells us that things are not awry.

Verlaine – as fast as they come, and at rapid speed. And never thinking twice. Always holding aloft the flag, always singing. Never letting go. And here where the sun does not dive, and the hairclips do not falter. There will be an inching to record.

Just which way do you want to come? Just which way do you want the barge to move? There is a new type of sound, it embarks on a lonely road, and knows that the help that is needed is not far away. Please come, you are needed.

Verlaine – never seeing the crossroad because of the trees. Never being one to see things out of the eye's edge. We are here for you, up and around-a-bouts. We will come when we are needed. And then, as if by magic, an unusual piece of luck.

Coming closer to the heart of things. Coming closer, and not giving in. We are like the bandits, closing in. We are like sound reasoning that gathers pace. We are like that which has no life, no life, but only to give. And then, a seed.

Verlaine – hanging closer together, than ever. Knowing only the sound of drums, and the sound of pipes. Be the weather, but only for a moment. Be the tempest, it will send a shock through you. I have longed to be with you, but that will not hurt, will it?

Harbours, and troubadour winging. What was once night, is now the breaking of solstice whims, and concubine hearts. There listens a greater longing than has ever been seen. And then, without care, a sense that we belong.

Verlaine – what is this? What is this on the wind of things? There is more of the pointed ex-change, that we ever had thought to feel. And then, when the light leaves our eyes, a festival of tumbling remembrance, as if the state was real.

Pointing towards the door, we get up to leave, and know that once in a September bliss, there comes the rite of passage. This rite is not ours alone, but we must see into it from time to time, just so our passage resembles that from which we were.

Verlaine – do you come in pointed mass? Is yours the fasting before the feast? Is yours the lining of the day, and all that will come to pass? There are noises where there should be silences. There are wings where there should be winds.

What do we say, when saying has said enough? What do we accomplish, when to accomplish is sit still for an hour? And then, with more than the oak to guide us, there is a rush of blood that augurs no relief. But we will continue.

Verlaine – do you sense what I sense? Do you feel what I feel? It is like the message has got-ten a task hard too little, and come back stronger than ever. There are things we must not dis-miss, for all our labour. And here, where we believe, we see again.

The tackle and the trope – augmenting the play from back stage. Come now we are not to lin-ger, we are only to stay when we are told to do so. And now, let us!

Verlaine – how do you feel? How do you say your name? Do you believe in things to come? Have you heard of the trace and the whimsy? There are things we must do. There are things we must do to tame the wildness from your eyes. Verlaine.

The coming months may see a drop in input from the clouds. But why is that? It is as if the moisture in the sky is not enough to propel the vastness of things. And then, what do we have? We have the sky to be as itself, what's more.

Verlaine – I have heard, oh wise man, that the trees are here for laughter, and the ravine is here for adventuring. And nothing else must save us, until the wilderness has a boast to go further than any ghost in any ship!

Destroying the passage, down to the last vestige. And here, where we pride ourselves in nothing less, there is a tenderness that harks back to when we were of the north, and the south had come to play. But these are but memories,

Verlaine – hanging in close, there envisions a stead to take us. And when we are with the one hundred or so patrons, we will raise our plates to the sky, and have as our task master the believing in side-glimpsed hope, and weathervanes.

There is like the need we once had to be at the behest of fate. And then, without a care, there is a new found whispering, that gently calls in the world for a look, and then says, yes I will help. Are you the one to help my Verlaine?

Verlaine – why in this domain does the light flick on with such vulgar repetition? There are times when the sand will not fall. I have come back to see things as they are. I have seen the true score, and its succession is still to come.

Beginning to travel that little bit faster. Hanging on so that we don't know our own name. Being that which believes in many things. Being the salt on the ground, and the hedge of the hedgerows. Never feeling, always wanting. Yes.

Verlaine – can we even see ourselves in this light? Can we believe in things unknown? Is this more than we can see? Is this what we say everything has come too? The nest is not on display. The limb it rests on cannot hear.

Having the most amazing adventure, and not being sure of its dimensions. Being the one to look back, only to be jerked forward. There are new things to see. New larks to whisper in agreeance with. New times to have with old friends.

Verlaine – do we not see you, my friend? You are the way of the whistle. You are the longed for step in the dark. Your pinions do not lift, but catapult forward. Your signs only point the di-rection to go, but that is more than the rest of us.

Catching a sight of what is next, and not believing. Always with the surest hand, we wait. Al-ways with the sight of angels do we tread. Always living across from the moon, and not know-ing the distance. We will come, that much is written.

Verlaine – a gall to wish away. A single sentence written as long as a book. What is in the midst of it, and that cannot sway. What we say when we jump a little higher.

Cramming in the stable for another look. Being one not to fake it. Desperation in the vision, but not in the hands. See the swinging we do, it helps immeasurably. Do not disturb as we have, there is a sweetness amongst it.

Verlaine – do you want to? Do you want to be the way we all are? Is this a dream you might have had, and then forgotten? There can only be a knight to parcel, and then, around. I have felt like something in the way of it, but not quite.

Listening to see if there is a disclaimer in the wind. Listening to see if the wharves are ready. Never fearing, always fearless, you come to us from on high with a new dimension in the gist of it. Come what may, I will feel.

Verlaine – is this a solemn rite? Does this rite right wrongs? Can we be that little bit further on, down the road, before we sell our souls to the highest bidder? And then, in the waters, behind the throne, there remains something strong!

Forests with no trees. Seas with no waves. A softening place that lets in the breeze. And then, for another time, a catching in the lineament, that does not sting. What is there that is left to do? What is there that is left to say?

Verlaine – a message to the family, do come in. We are of peace and leisure, and we know the price of pain. There is a mighty rush that sheaves as it lulls, that transpires as it loves. Do not depend on the weary, their journey abounds.

There are things that don't cross. There are things that have as their guide all the weathering of the sky. Do not be one to shirk the desire we all have to treasure the wonderment of things. This is not to say something which is not.

Verlaine – are you the one apt enough to sense the change, and overcome it? Do you see for yourself all the intransigencies of life, and come again for more? Is there a stealing of wine, one that has no tower?

Now come, there is still time. Now come, the heart is in the hearth. The heart is without dearth. There is an amazing symbiosis hidden here. And then, when the caustic and blue combine, there is an amazing reluctance to bend.

Verlaine – what is most at stake, is not the sand which burns, nor the righteous that alleviates, but that which comes in fire and ice, to heat, and to cool. There is never anything more than this. We must not waste.

Holding on, so that our clothes are not in disrepair. Holding on, so that the wind will not take us. Holding on, so that we may love the centre once more. There is a fashioning of winter jackets, high in the collar, room for the shirt collar too.

Verlaine – There is a mess the size of a horse here. But how do we clean it? With staunch re-luctance, but with the farcical in our hands, off we go. Is there room for more? Is there room for one last adhesion? Let us hope so.

Gathering for the season. Gathering for what is left. There is a new voice here, let it sound! Why have we not seen the treasures that lie within? We will.

Verlaine – coming to, do you see us also? All the way forward, all the way back. Do you wit-ness skies made of grey, skies made of yellow? Is there something tempting you Verlaine, tempting you into the sink? Don't stop now!

Belittling the noise that is made by the heard. Belittling what is made in times of darkened ma-laise. What is this we seek? Do we seek the circumference of the square? Do we seek the no-body who hovers bright?

Verlaine – are you right for travelling? Do you spend time for archery? Do you seek whatever it is that only harbours life, as it does decay? There is often no time left to see the wellspring at its full disposal. We must not shirk.

A bastion, and then the cold. One more visage to maintain, and then through. What is more, is never enough. What we see, can only bind us. What we sense, is never in the untold. Be the myth, and the flame will be yours.

Verlaine – more than the half of it. We are here to liberate. And what can we say, but all that is. What can we believe, in the distance that is thronging. Do we believe, when things are scrambled. This much is said in the dark.

Gaining in generosity, each day that passes, each day that is not in dispute. Feeling like the sage, and having him beckon dearly. We will not fathom the abyss anymore. And then, without accord, or convenience, there is some upside to the night.

Verlaine – are you the one to laugh, to laugh the loudest? Do you strengthen yourself on barbs of the everyday? Is this what we come for, to sense the night is upon us? I have never dreamt of things so real. I have never seen of things this way.

And then, without the kind of favour to be sought from any moon, there is now a seeming in-tractable impasse in the wood. Time goes, but does it stay when it is needed? The sense we have to let things settle will keep us in good stead.

Verlaine – does your fire reign down on settlements of wood, settlements of card? Is this thing called life here, and for the loving? There is a nice place to start from, we will see it if we can. But what is the point of the daylight if not for the night?

Gaining a foothold in things, things un-chimed. What is there in the way of it, that we do not know the distance? There is a kind of reticent joy here, that only believes in itself at certain times. Can we find its camaraderie, and bring it forth?

Verlaine – there are troubles not depicted on the scale, so we must gather ourselves again, and fall in line to the chosen few. Never bring back the score, it is a thing that holds itself dear. And then, without reason, a simplicity takes hold.

Mixing in the remnants of times past, and times present. Time future is nothing other than the soil that grows a thousand trees. Be a remnant of times past, and yours will be a beacon unto the hills, unto the day. And then, a vanishing act! And then, yes!

Verlaine – what is it we have left? What is it that the sky light is want to judge? There is more of the sound of things, less of the arc of things. Come now – away!

Basking in something else – we find our way through the litmus test of life. And now, when the strength of a thousand horses, there goes a vacuum in search of love. Do not be surprised, there is adventure ahead. I am one to see the straight ahead.

Verlaine – is this what we seek? Is this what we need to be whole again? Is this what we trav-erse in times of need? Do we set ourselves up, to once again fall? In this, there are many truths, many ways of seeing things. Be still, it won't hurt to be.

Fathering something more than the welling of all things great. There is a chance to sail the winter's abyss, and do what we have always said we would. And that is fly at the lasting edge. Come now, we must not tire, tire of the wholesome and the mess.

Verlaine – come at the window like it was a good friend. Lock onto the way of it like a cry in the night. Do not fathom a release from the bonds that bind. There is a sense we can make it if we have the strength. Do we have the strength? Yes we do.

The prism of language, refracting all we experience, bending the light of knowledge. Are we free to use this parlance, to fit in tight corners of the tenacity of this fight, and this myriad of ways to be? Come now, we must not devalue ourselves.

Verlaine – is this what the treasure is all about? Is this what we have struck up as a friend in waiting? There is a time for all of us to gather, and wonder at sparks unseen. There are wishes that know only the round, and then are let go of.

Ongoing, and in reach. We settle for the round, and know that our time is short. Be the wan-derer, and the wandering of fireflies will be tenacious. Be the suitor, and what will follow will endear a nation. Listen closely, it will be in your favour.

Verlaine – offset, and to the right. Offset and to the left. Just offset, and then bear what comes. There is a new set of stalactites to wander through. Do not enjoy yourself so, there is much work to do. Much work, and even some pleasure.

The time it takes to rattle a dust bin is the same time it takes to win a race. And then with food for the taking, we are set in our ways, and know that the sound of quintessential basking to be true. Never resist our call, it lures.

Verlaine – committed to the call, but the call for what? Is it the call for the ages? Is it the call for the city? Is it the call for the country; the call of the forests? There is never anything more than this. Never anything more than that envisioned from the start.

Do you see how the swallow flies? Do you see how the moisture in the ends of it freezes? There is almost something we don't allow. And what is that? It is the chiming of winter winds. But why not? They are so lovely.

Verlaine - on the way there, we took a funny path that led nowhere. We had to retrace our steps, and on the way back we came across a tomb stone, one with no writing on it. We puz-zled for a while, and then fell back on our path – and away.

Desperately seeking respite, we lurch forward, and again, seek something beyond ourselves – something that does not lurch, or have its fibres catch. Yes.

Verlaine – why is this here? Why is the sand so pernicious, and not what we expected? Is this the way we lead our lives, without the sense we have to send the ship aflutter? There is more than a way forward here, more than we had hoped.

Coming in the time it takes to raise a bar. Having the need to drive the carriage that one further mile. There is nothing like this in all the world. There is nothing like this anywhere. We will see what happens. It will most likely rain.

Verlaine – having the spell cast, but not knowing its potency. Wishing for things to be settled, but only for the day. What is it that we seek? What is the time it takes to rattle a bushel, and have it flake? There are times to be, and this is one of them.

Having the sense to move to the side. Having the wherewithal to settle old scores. And then, when we knew what was here, we would not languish any more, and would up and move to the motion of the wind. Come through, it will suit.

Verlaine – what we saw is not enough to lay a pretence for the song, nor a wanting for the day. And here, where the noise of longing spares a windswept glance, there mires not the farce, but withholding of winter digress. This will do.

Holding the banner aloft, the street can never know its name. But what is it? It is a further lov-ing embrace, that holds itself in good stead. What must we say, to weather the scene as its stands? We must say nothing, but be still, and be filled.

Verlaine – do you have the hallow to let it be? Is this where we live? Is this where the train travels fastest? I have never known such trepidation, but only for a while. And here where the mast is in full sail, a sense the night has that things are not awry.

Catching on the seam of things. There is more than our fair share of troubles. But what of the millipede's march, as she wanders in arcs of golden thread. There is now a time for rejoicing, and a time laying down weapons, and searching in full.

Verlaine – what has cast its thread, is enough to beckon the withstanding of a lying down that has no flecks for the dismantled, nor holding for the night-time and her embrace. We have not seen the likes of it in many a year.

What is not forced upon us, is something we cannot surmise. And then, like a worn out map, the tools we have come forward to let us use them in great sways. Do not be one to jettison the harbour before due course. There will be time.

Verlaine – being one to laugh last. Being one to settle into things. Being the chance, and having it rub. In the time it takes to feather an arrow, we will have come, and set the stone's throw going. In this we are sharp, and still reeling.

Found on the stage, but what is the moisture of it all, that cannot be surpassed? There is now a sense that when we come, we come for the good, and know it to be a thing worth teething. And the sound we make when we no longer move?

Verlaine – come for me, my prince! Come for the dawn, but also come for me. There are treasures here worthy of the sand. So do not pretend, just come.

Bringing forth the bounty. There are things we must do, and things that must remain undone. And here, where the great is in mire, there is an untold land of nice and refined spirit. And then, when we find our heart, our soul, we will prefigure.

Verlaine – have you not seen the way? Have you not seen the troupe as it comes waylaid? There is a tremendous boon to be mistaken here. But what of the rest of it? This much patrols the shores. And then, without so much as a motion, we make it!

Two-way, and three-way, never a chance, always a chance. And then without the mould cov-ered books to send on the path, there is a fire dance to cover the chances at being, and being sampled. But what of the troupe? We will find a way.

Verlaine – never before seen! Never seeing the light of day. What we cannot figure is the time it takes – how many years is this? How many years in the mists of time? There only takes one to dream away! And then when we settle things, the mast.

Almost willing to come. But that is not enough! We must be fully sure, and then come as if volition is not wanting. That is the way to do it! The test of things always resides in the water. This is pivotal. And then, the sound we hear, is nothing other than fate.

Verlaine – always on the hunt. Always ready to chase. But what is it that we need, but nothing? What is it we have, but all? There are things that we must not do without. But that is what the sands of time are for, to diminish, ever quicker.

Without the need to be, there is nothing left to see. And then, when the barbs of time have had their say, we will listen like never before. And truthfully, this is not the way to stand, and in this formulation, lies the treasure of the sand.

Verlaine – what more do you feel, when love is conquered, and the new land is up for measuring? We see the place inside ourselves as we never again patrol the coastline. What is there left, when the chance at forever is here?

The coquette, and the lines in the sidewalk. What made us frivolous is thanks to nothing, oblivion. The stance we all took has paid dividends. But what of that, when the makeshift holds rings through every fibre of the desert? We will come again.

Verlaine – do you believe once again? Is this your solemn rite? Can we tell of the outer ocean, where we are in the world? I have known places deep, and curses weep, and here where the stand of whispers in the night is strongest, we come.

I hope I never forget the ring that behoves the dawn. The things which hide the sway are a blessing and a night-thrift. Be that which is not the sand, and we will see more than all. Do you come for the door-strings, and all that will come to pass?

Verlaine – let us write as we want to write! And then, without time to pursue the mist we will gather to the horizon, and know it for the first time. I am one not to recollect the distance be-tween this land and the next. For more of the adventuring, come!

What is in the cradle, is not what we thought. And here where we see left over clover, we reminisce about times gone by, and think ourselves lucky.

Verlaine – happiness comes in many forms, but none like this. When one has come like this, in a fashion that does not question the dawn, there arises new faith, and new longing, and new treasures to bequeath. What is left – nothing!

Never in a distance does the ring sing tried and true. Never do the building blocks of life see themselves anew. And then as we atone for the ravaging of time, there is a chance to sit amongst the embers, and reckon on the fabric of the whole itself.

Verlaine – there are pieces of land that do not draw fibre from the bricks of solicitude. But here, where we have found the recompense that we all need, all need to challenge by, there is here a new simulacrum to fill our days by. Yes, fill.

Always bowing, never bestowing, until the end of things. There is here more space than we could have hoped for. And when the dream follows its path through to the end, there is means of hope and residue, hope, and the triumph of will!

Verlaine – what do we see with our vision? What do we see with our new need to fly! There is no lack of motivation here, no trundle in the dark, no sense we have that lives have not been lost. And here, where sound is like a vapour, we sing.

Causing a ruckus, there bleeds a mighty beast. We cover its wound, and then check our direction. There lives in the eyes of some a dream-like omen, an oneiric, if you will, an oneiric block to live by. What have you seen, my poor man!

Verlaine – hop in here! To the very end! Know not what hit us! And then, as if a light had been turned on, something to harness the weather of the years. Come now, we must not feel levity, the occasion is too solemn. And that's where it comes!

Almost willing to breathe, the sands of the hour glass rise in unison, and tremble out. What do we say, now that the cloud is in motion? We stare, and walk on, not knowing what to do. I have a suggestion – run in a straight line, do not look back!

Verlaine – have you seen yourself lately? Have you seen what it is that beckons to the mist? Have you seen what it is that harbours new nights? There are courses of action from this point to that, and it is here, that we see our sands appear.

Wishing to live upside down, and right and way up – but which do we choose? Do we choose to be in love with things? Or do we fall out with things? I do not know. But in this is an inkling of what is to come. Always tenacious, forever dreaming.

Verlaine – are you one to be like the wind? To be insatiable to the left of things? And then when together we yearn, then all that will be will be, and all that will canonise will say – Yes, and believe once again in the strength of things. How about that!

Forests, surging with forgetfulness. Springs bubbling this way and that. What is new is never old. What has the sun, is never of the moon. We should not forget ourselves here, we should only have a head for lounging. This much is true.

Verlaine – are you one to die another death for us? Are you to gather yourself for another as-sault at Prince of Poets? Let us steel ourselves.

Frivolous, and wanting to change. There is never enough in the forest to placate. Be true, the time is not wasting. And here where we see ourselves again in a mirror with no salt, we will find a new way to be, opposite the lines that are drawn.

Verlaine – what have you seen, that we have not? What is it that drives you still? Is there a place for the weary in your load? Do you find yourself in the wool of things? What is this we speak of? I have come for the weather, now let us steel ourselves.

The last trace of it, never again thought of. What is left of us, has nothing of the rotund. There are times in amongst it that we feel of Latin, and of verses, but together? There are things here that never say a word. Let us hear them.

Verlaine – constantly shining, and never dismayed. The reprehension of days is nothing short to bargain by. And then, when we are enough endured, a sort of sanctity lives on in the wonder and the thrall. Do not be dismayed, nothing can hurt.

Gaining ground, hoping for the next approbation to transfix. Love, and be loved, that is the motto at the end of it all. Nothing short of the standard we bear, there is life, and there is life. Do not come swimming, we must walk the distance.

Verlaine – do you see what is there; over there, in the garden of sweet perfume? It is as if we could not swing the latest notion. Be terrible, I know you can be. But what of the festooned and the rivalry? What of that to keep us in the hallow.

Never before seen. Never before witnessed. Always growing, never seeming to care. What is that we say? What is that we do? I have never heard the saying articulated so well. And then, when we know our own life as well as others!

Verlaine – come now, let us not fight, let us be dreamy, and comfort each others sorrow. There are things we can do to relinquish the hold we have on hate. But what is that which holds us back? Not much to say, but that is okay.

Gaining in momentum, the skies reach out for the triumvirate and see themselves not lost, but gained in strength and aplomb. Never weeping, always feigning. Never to see what is left. Come, and be what is more. Just come and be!

Verlaine – is this your way, the way home? Is this what you do to sail the open sea? Is this what you do? I am sure, there can be nothing like this anywhere. The time it takes to wander is not our time, but theirs. Hold on, we will ride.

Oven, and pincers, oven and shadows. There moisture of
the skies does not surprise. And then, when we love so
much, so much of what we do, there is a centre piece in the
gesticula-tions of the roundabouts, and life renews again.

Verlaine – nothing more of the sound, the sound that makes
us cringe. There is like a water in our eyes that has no
bearing to give, nor co-ordinate to swing by. Love and see
through the trees, that covers the whole we live in.

Having a chance to breathe, and then, seeking in close.
Neither here nor there, nor up nor down. What we wager for,
to have as our solace the wind.

Verlaine – have you seen the show? Have you witnessed all
that is? Is this the way we delve into things? Come now, we
must not flinch, we must be all we can be, and more. What
do we say, when saying is at an end? We say much more,
and then?

Cockerels, and sea shells, the naming of the sense of it.
What we have given for the strumpet and the lark. Heaven
knows what I have been through. Longing, and the lost
annunciation. Holding onto the sky, and knowing your
desire.

Verlaine – Have you seen todays liturgy? Full and there.
Never receding, always believing. There is nothing more we
can say! But what of this, that ums and ars to a point
beyond. What is there to say, when to say, is never to
conquer.

Gathering pace, we see what is ahead. Distance and the
wire – distance and amplitude. There can be nothing more
than this. There can always be more. What have we seen,
but the chime as it stands. The chime of all time.

Verlaine – loving the assault on open ground. Loving the certain life we have, and all its ech-oes and chambers. Do we see something now, we hadn't seen before? It is something of the ethereal, and hangs on by might and wisdom.

Away in the midst of it, there comes a sound, a sound that we have no liking against. And now, what we dream for most in temper, is aloft and proud – there is nothing like it, the cut and thrust of symbiosis and all that she can give.

Verlaine – are you the underling who about faces in times of greyish doubt? There is more here than the tempest has shown, but what of the night, and all she forestalls? There is now a new sense to old wounds that cannot be what we truly want.

Having the vase, and seeing it through. There is now a testament to a furrowed brow, that does only see the sea, and everything that comports to be the linen in the cupboard. Do not dry your eyes, there is only what is left.

Verlaine – catching on to the sea shell is only what we have always wanted. And now, when the diatribe rings true, do we see the valve for what it is, and that is a thing of beauty. Do not lie here, there is no room. We have chastened the wanderer.

And then, without surprise, a new sense that we can make a life of it. Do not come forth, there are messengers on the wind. And here, where the ladle and the spoon dance in unified recognition, here, oh here, there is time for the righting.

Verlaine – hold onto that thought, there is more room here that we knew. And then, with strings made of iron, the

bending of winter wind knows no light. What is this, I hear
you say? What is this that does not transcend, but moves
slowly?

For all the while, we are being ensconced in brightest noon.
Forever told to wait, forever here and now. And then with a
modicum of desire, we say with briefest respite, there comes
a time that sees no dance, but is in the frame.

Verlaine – what has left, is not the partridge, nor the
presence to sing, but the way we see these things. And
then, like a motivated owl, we see ourselves anew.

The moisture in the way of things, is not what we had in
mind. But that is okay, we always adapt and curtail what it is
that keeps us moving. I write from the heart, but is that
enough? There are changes, and chanceless breaths that
only breathe.

Verlaine – there is now a chance to see things a straight. To
see things as they should be seen, not as they are, but as
we see them to be. Holding onto the web, we now see more
than the time it takes to racquet up a storm. Yes, that is it.

And now, with no more than a side-glimpsed hope, there is
luck in the wind of it. Luck at the story of the nice and
reposed. I am now what they say I am. I am now the
dizzying height, the lowest low, and everything in between.
Come and stay.

Verlaine – do you wonder what we find, when the light
cannot dim, and the treasures of sol-stice picking linger in
unjust ease, and the night-time has only itself to blame!
There are cus-toms that only betoken sense. But it will be
here.

Holding on, like the nuances of a worn out fate. There are chances to breath here, and breath well and deeply. The nice invective we have shallowed is no more. But what of the beauty of the hills? It is here, and will never leave.

Verlaine – are you the one who is a living edge to all that passes, and all that suits a rye belly. In the mist, there is time, more so now we have the faith of things. Do not forestall the day-dreaming messages, they will come. Just be here – yes!

And there we are. And there we go. What is more, we love the very thought of it. Everything comes down to this. This magical partition in the sand. There is here a reckoning that has no might. A silence that has no shafts to bear. We are here.

Verlaine – never have you seen so much, and born so little. There is so much to tell of, and we must tell it. But what of the storyline, prim and proper? Only in the strength of a thousand iron clad warriors can we truly see the venture.

Never in a thousand dreams have we seen this. The titan goes cold for a holiday, and the weathering of business as usual. We are not ones to see our furthest in the gloom. But that is okay, until closing of shores, we sail.

Verlaine – gosh, and darn it, have you a keepsake? Is your ritual a new sense of things to come? Is the sandal in the park yours? Do you persist in times of yore? Is the magnet a thing to be reckoned with? Do you store your beliefs above your head?

Listening to the dawn, we labour in times unknown. We labour, and know the features to be wanting. Do not drive

your carriages here, they are fully in charge of themselves. I
knew not what to do, except linger by the grave.

Officially, a saved life. It only takes one, and then a new life
is born. What can we say, but the timing is right. We will not
see the likes of this for some time. Come and be the trilogy
to the night, there is something more we must say!

Verlaine, do you see ourselves aright, when aid is at the
beck and call? Is this the tempest that bleeds solemn oaths.
There is a magnificence here. Touch it.

Having the test, and beating it down. Feeling like we never
have before. Arching our backs, and seeing them turn.
There is now a place, a place I run too. It covers me in
sweetness, and in delectable charm. I will have no other
way. None.

Verlaine – the size of this distance is not insurmountable. It
is something we tend to in our dreams, and in our desires.
Do not wander here, fate is at hand, and has an angry tone.
But wait, what is this? Is it the sand we seek? I believe so.

Almost grabbing on, there is a time for motive force, and
time for things undone. There is a chance we can do what
we have always wanted. And here, where the noise of the
dandelions do not drown out the noise of the bees, silence.

Verlaine – what do we say now, now that the oasis is given
to the daylight? What do we want of things, that cannot be
wanted again. There are laughs, and there are wantings. But
what of the show, that has no compunction, no rattle bag of
life?

There can never be a wanna be haven. And in this not place, there resides a feeling that the time we have left is not strained at all. And then, without the slightest care, there is a scary transcendence that has life as it has tears.

Verlaine – The meaning to it all, has the whimper of a worn out butterfly. And what do we say, when this butterfly chases the field, and never relinquishes the sayings of dirt. We will come again, and find out what is said, and then, unsaid.

The caustic, and the whishing bell. And when we arise, a new type of being. One that has only flight. There is nothing prouder than a victory sought for in the wings. And now, we will come again, with resplendent array – fully decked, and composed.

Verlaine - what is this I hear you say? What is this, in the lines that do not drag? There can be nothing more than the April day noon-tide, which never relinquishes its heart and its determination. Fellow rubric, and simple things arrived. We will come.

And now, for the chains that no longer bind, there is here a meaning, and a waiting, and a seeing through. Please come now, there is truth in the rafters, and sense in worn out trees. We have never seen a great fight. Let us speak.

Verlaine – have you notice the round in the play? Have you been that thing that does not waylay? There are tempests that shirt no front. And then, when we race, a new speed gathers for us, and we try once again to herald in the light of day.

Forests that stand. Never before witnessed gravity. A new turn with old speed. All the more ready, ready to shout. We will come again. We will come again, and know the place of it to be something that the options of time itself cannot explain.

Verlaine – There is a feeling that I once knew – I haven't thought of it in the time of ages. But what this thought gives me is the power to overcome any obstacle. Any divot it the road. Any unsafe passage. One thought. One outcome.

A chance, a chance to rub hands with the best. There is now a ruby red in the stable of our love. Do not colour the sand. Hope lives here, and will not depart.

Verlaine – what is there left? What is there left, that no gull could eat? And now, when the traipsing of winter foibles comes to its apex, there lies a road ahead – we must follow, and in following, hear the rain on tin rooves. We will come.

Harrowing, and in the fold. The things we meet along the way, are a trouble and a fathoming. Do not be alarmed, my sweet, there are distances that everyone must traverse. Come now, we are there, do not believe otherwise!

Verlaine – hanging out to dry, the votive mass is here at hand. There will be time enough for liturgy now that the fawns of the weak have become strong. There is now nothing more to do. The song, and the sweet, and the mischievous surrounds.

All the more reason to go to the bellows, and see what can be seen. There is a time to rush, and a time to be still. And everything in-between. There are now people to see, and talk to, and visit, and be strange with. The catacombs lie ahead.

Verlaine – something in the water has just occurred. Something roundabouts, and through and all about. I am sure that outcome is good. That much we can be assured of. Do not linger though, the sport of it does not belie the age.

Come now, what we thought was the meaning, is of course the sense. It is as if the rain just simply stopped falling, mid-flight. I have known many things, but never this. We can only say of it, that it is something we cannot renege!

Verlaine - do you run that extra indulgence? Is this what it takes to bear the load? Can we see what is in the window, and never look back? There are times when we are needing to go forwards, and times when we are needing to go backwards.

What is this now? This beat on drums of steel? There can only be the weather to remind us, remind us of the vantage we are on. But when there is now a harbour, where there was once sunshine, we will come again in mists of grey.

Verlaine – Come to the ready. Quick. And steel yourself for anger. And when the treasure and the import come again in succession, there is a sense that time itself will still the turning world. Do not abandon hope, we still have what is needed.

And then, without care, nor favour, there is a sense that the blocks of our heart will not now come any further. And this is where we find ourselves, in the midst of the grey of night, of the happenstance and the mile. Be brave, be strong.

Verlaine – have you not lost your shoe, my Verlaine? Where is it, and what does it symbolise? In the meantime we will walk, until walking is no more. The sense we have that the righteous and the bold linger in blinding light. Do come.

Gaining a foothold on the stars. We will have the notion that things are here for the keeping, and the solitude of the adventurer is one to melt berries on. And here, where the distance we once saw, is now no more, a tender hand, and then together.

Verlaine – the fanning of the gate, to let it open, and then, let us come through, is more than we could envision. But let us not hurry, we will see it through.

A graduated relief, that hears none of the gracious alert. But come now, there is here amongst us a fever pitch of rivalry, and a sense that no person can really touch it. Find the way home, and you will have a special undertaking. Find the way home.

Verlaine – are you the one to see to the heart within? Is this what we all seek – the heart with-in? There are charges of silk, and charges of clay. Which will we be, I hear you say? And then, with mouths opened to the sky, a sense we can make it.

Alright, it seems. Alright, and then through. What is the newness of it all? What do we do to gather the rose petals from the dawn? Is it something we have always known what to do? And then, a charging gait, that stills nothing, but itself.

Verlaine – casting forward, and around, and then through, we see the mischief of the fowl as a language to me and you, to never give in, and never say no. We cannot be the weather here, in a weatherless land, there is only the stark reminder of the times.

Ageless, and seeing, both with sand, and with glass. There is a feeling that the goal is here, and the dregs of the land are no more. What is this district in which we walk? Is it new to be on the side of the walkway that is straight, or taken?

Verlaine – the kindness we saw from the stranger, is all that is needed to get us there. I am one never to tire, but that is okay, there is no need to. We are a gasp, and a tattle, and only half of which is true. There is now before us, hope!

The chance we have is like a wind in solemn trees, that dare not doubt the way forward. And here, where the mistletoe does not miss, a sentience is born behind the stick in the sand. It is here to guide, and to feel – feel away across, and through.

Verlaine – there is nothing left of the old, and everything of the new – but what of it? What of the semblance of rhyme and repetition? We seek a new version in times of fastidious care, that no longer harness that sun as she burns us the night sky.

A flight, and a cooing and all that remains. Hoping for care, and hoping for the remnants of love, we do not seek the way of it under distant canopies, or distant shores. The cascading of a waterfall is not the sound we had hoped. But come!

Verlaine – is this the way we move, in syncopated abandon, in most solemn redress? There is a silence here that only the noise of harps could ever believe in. And then, at an angle, the joy we seek, and the due course of events.

Wishing, hoping, seeing through it all to the other side – never finding the screw, but having the right to believe. What is that we seek, but everything we have desired. Is this where we find ourselves, once again, in times dark ease, and random events.

Verlaine - the timbers have failed to rot! The engine is now ready to be driven! What we have now is the sense that time is at a standstill, and the way around is back on its knees. The col-our of his eyes. The colour of his eyes does not sleep.

Forgetting the stillness, and knowing the farm to be ready, there is a new way to see things – a new way to be. What is the way of it, but solidly up!

Verlaine – are you the happiness I seek? Are you in the playground of love, and there, sporting your lair for all that it is worth? There are messages from afar, and in them, we find fractions of a long lost age – when help procured help!

There is a strength in these words I give to you. I do not take credit for them, they are not mine to call mine. But what is left is utter mischief! And that I feel has come full circle. Do not listen to my words, but have the latest from the well!

Verlaine - conscious of the might of things, there is a sign post written in the sky, that says no you must stay, or, no you must go. And in this embrace we carry on, until the daylight does not shine, and the humidity is not a thing to shame.

No discord in the chime of it. No discord in the miles we teach. No discord in the water that weeps! Having the happiness of the journey return, and then feeling its circumference like the back of a hand. Journey forward. Yes, come.

Verlaine – are you the secret of the two? Does your memory eat the dust of excess? Do you need telling once more, so that energy flows in the tree tops. Do you fancy something colder, more than the tundra, more than the snow?

Virtually nothing here has settled. Nothing to wade through, nothing but the intrepid adventurer. So who goes there? Who straddles the dune? Who believes in ravines? There is never a cost too great – isn't there? No there isn't.

Verlaine – does your spell in the woods ring true? Is there life in these parts? I do not know; some, perhaps. Where do we sing from then? Where is the twilight and its ilk? We are longing to know, and to feel, and who knows what else. Come.

Fortunate in one sense, and not in others. But that is okay, the sand comes in peculiar forms here, and knows what the daylight has to offer, and that is much. Due to the rattle bag and the rambunctious, levity will be afforded to the remote.

Verlaine – what is white? What is black? What do we see when we see both? Hands to hearts, and what we see when we look? There is never a prudent guess at what is most precious? Do not tend to the rhyme, it is meaning we want here.

Cascading down abandoned waterfalls, there is something in the grace of it that lets a little burn come through. A slowly receding fault line, that covers the ages in silk. What is there here that we cannot see? What is the irruption we do not experience?

Verlaine – among the wind chimes and aging poplars, there is time to just be alone. And in that time, we come forward as one to help. But what is lying in wait for the adventurous spirit, nothing but all. All that chains can see as broken.

Gaining in on the frost, and having the hoary nature of things listen, there is a gateway here, beyond the toss of a coin, and the rubric of the quintessential, a thing that never leaves. Come for the show, stay for glad tidings. We will come.

Verlaine – do you see yourself in the mirror, not that the show has gone? Is there nothing left now, but the drone of work? There is nothing, just as we like it.

Reaching forward and through, and into what lies next. The story remembers itself from the times before, and then reiterates itself again for the glory of the mischief maker and the little residual that has no lie. Come and see us again, yes.

Verlaine – there is nothing worthy of this catch, this catch of the sea. There is only what we thought would never come, and never be besieged. Wanting and wishing and only seeing what is right. Come now we are falconed pressed. Come now.

Listening to the scales of time to cherish every last moment, we sense something magical in the wind of things. There is a sort of sensing but not doing, a sort of levity that does not tinder, nor folk to shine on indefinitely. Feel the way. Yes.

Verlaine – opposite the water and the life dispenser, there lies a new type of meandering. And here, where the things we thought were for certain, were here and then, now. There is nothing to know beyond this. Beyond this pall, and shawl.

Lost in the embrace, feeling like we should. There is life here, life in amongst it, and then what do we find, but the newest of the new. What is more, we do not lag behind, anymore! That is what we saw here years ago. Months ago, years ago.

Verlaine – are you the one who simply offers? Are you the one who catches on the wind, catches on the sail? Is this were we go, into the depths of it, into the snow. And where we are headed, nobody knows, except the counterpoint. And how far is that?

Reaching into the ever mist, there is a place beyond places, a time beyond time. And here where withholding is a might and a distance, there comes things again, things that only rever-berate in tune to the chosen. Be one with the clime, it will suit.

Verlaine – do you have your fill again? Is this the way you climb, nestled away in the warmth of it? I see you sustain yourself in pure white, in pure clay. There is nothing left of us, except the time it takes to bend bamboo into shapes. We will march!

Gaining in shafts of light – there is a tempest to dissolve all tempests. And here, where the night does not shine, there is a kind of remittance that allows the moon's light to shine again. And here, where the sun does its dance – forever and again.

Verlaine – there are trees here, that bark no resolve. There are new tensions that embark upon old novices. Do not find that way here, it is closed off. But that is okay, a solemn way finds itself from the mire, and uses itself once again to sense the day.

Furtive steps. Steps that lead nowhere, except out to sea. There is in us something that beg-gars belief, to come full circle, with belief again. Are you the one to come into the mission to sense the land that lies beneath. Come now, we must!

PAUL VERLAINE

Verlaine – cascading in light colours, never really seeing until we are at the bottom. Never really knowing what is what. And then, a light flashes, and what we saw as behind ourselves, is in front, and what was beside us to the left, is too the right.

Foraging through the distance, there are new times that live in old deviances. There is some-thing here, that we cannot pick, that we can only hold hands with.

Verlaine – coming into the light. What do you say we do? What do you say we know? The merriment will be a semblance of outer kindness. And here, where the sand is at its zenith, there will be something more to do. And something more to say.

Classically in the time it takes. There is here something we don't understand, something that the world treasures, and that we have missed. But what is this thing? What is this thing we have missed? We may never know. Until tomorrow.

Verlaine – there is motion where there should be stillness, and stillness where there should motion. But here, where stars are at their brightest, there will be a welcoming and a homecom-ing, to beat all homecomings. What is there left. Nothing!

A house in the trees. A house on the plains. A house anywhere, and then, well there. I don't know much about this, but in the semblance of the way, there is a map, and there is written all that can be written. Never forsake the wind. Yes, the wind.

Verlaine - do you see what we would all like to see? And that is glad fall at the winter crest! And now, without the slightest bit of hesitation, there is something to look forward to, some-thing to rest our hat on at the end of the day.

Forging through like an engine in the dark. Giving what is fruitful, and knowing it to entice. There are lands that have no respite, and here, where the dance is half done, the truisms of fate lie in blissful slumber over all that comes next.

Verlaine – do you hear me? Do you hear the sound of dreams in the night? They are like a fresco in amongst the embers. But still it survives! Do you catch yourself from time to time making faces at the moon? We will be here for you!

Never mind the daylight, there are things to be seen here, that have as their sense all the guile and wonder of adventure, as we know it. Never send us to sleep too soon, there is something we must do. And here, where we are laden, again. Again.

Verlaine – do the blinds help you see? Do the wondrous creatures of the well leap fairly from our castle – a castle that is now in ruin, and as such, has beauty; beauty like never before. Why is that you think? That we must come to ruin to attain beauty?

Forests near and far. Forests that arch their backs to get away. Forests that hear their past as a murmuring in the breeze. Something that lets us in, for a chance at forever. Be the bold in-souciance, and all will come before you. Yes, be that.

Verlaine – are you the one who sings a mighty song? Are you dirtiest when you are hungry? Do tales told about you ring true? Is this where we are going, straight up? I can believe in no other thing. But what of this? What of the trails that ford no injury?

Catching some climbing before we depart. Catching some well earned rest before the festivi-ties. Am I going too hard here? We will tell if the future will have me! And then, masquerades, as a planet on the sun. Be free with it, it won't hurt.

Verlaine – in the meantime, we have the languishing of the daylight, that affords more than the hiccup chance, one that lays in spades, and then!

Having the courage to do what is best. Being that thing that laughs first. There is now a chance at real insistence. Now at last, the figure of our speech. We come down from our height, and use this might to start a fire, and then put it out.

Verlaine – do you spot yourself in the mire, but whirl yourself around so you are not seen! Is this the way of all things. Is this the way of the marsh, and the fellow, the fellowship of the mire. Do not get me wrong, there is nothing like this!

A messing with tendrils, tendrils that intertwine. We should let them go, and be as they are. Why must we be so intrepid? – Because we must, and we will not give up until our whole life is an adventure. Be that, and things will move in your honour.

Verlaine – do you sleep a thousand sleeps? Do you call on your name to save your very life? Is this what we foresaw in the web of it? Our own fate, that tells not of completion nor deliver-ance? There is a saying, which I now forget.

Granting hardship as a boon, this journey seeps with the reassurance of an age. What more do we have though, what more do we have, that never bushels a nuance. There are things we must not touch. And in not touching, go.

Verlaine – do you spend nights on your own, wishing for the tail to spark? And here, without a sound, there comes no night, and no gravity to call your own. Do not listen to the fairy tale of our lives. Here at heart there is more to see through.

Further and further than the sun. Never believing in something so large. Always finding out what is next. Believing in something special. A wish, and then a yesterday surprise. I am find-ing things worth keeping here, you never know.

Verlaine – having the verve to keep it. Having that something of worth. I will not believe in things of outside the circle, I will not believe in things in order of size. I have found something more, something greater than the rest. What is it?

Forests that know only weight. Dreams that harbour something more. What we have delivered is something in the middle. Do not sleep here – the doors are always open. And then, with the sails plump, we head towards the north sea.

Verlaine – A sensible tactic, one that never breaks. This is the way it goes, sometimes. Are we recruited into an unknown band. Is this the way we find things. There is no dismay here. Only excitement at the adventure. Let us go!

A new vice, one that sees only what we regret. A listening that calms. A corner stone that has fallen into favour. What we thought would never change. What we thought would only be what is left. Never reach for the deepest place. Take your time.

Verlaine – forging a hole in the deeper hole. Never crashing, always digging. And having such a time of it. There is more of a sending than a receiving here, but we must continue. We continue, and the roundabouts come with us!

Flashing before our eyes. We stand upright, and beneath the sands that carry us. We have more than our lives pertain. Do not be oblique here, there is time.

Verlaine – there is a place, a place with no heart. And we have been there, this place, this place with no heart. But the window to the soul, the face, the eyes, come unbidden through the ages. All we need is a glimpse, and we can see through.

Having the wind for the journey! Having what is best! There are wishes that should only be granted once! And then when we are sure of the tempest and its circumference, we never go back – we fight on, and on, and on.

Verlaine – a nice seal to be broken, one that lasts through the ages. Come now, and see the things that are remiss. We will write about them, and tell the world, you can have what you want. And now, a firmer reluctance to feel away to the stars.

Having the strength to continue, as we must. Having the strength, and seeing it through. There is a happenstance that rivals no ilk. There is a place amongst places, a place that carries forward. We will come, and come again.

Verlaine – Moving like we all should, one, two three. Moving like the sands never have. Moving in unison with the gaping soul. Having what is said. Desiring the path, but being dismayed at its difficulty. Holding on.

Shinning in thin blue air, the dust of a thousand whispers finds itself alone. And through it all, a nice touch of remembrance, that heralds all that can be heralded. What is this I hear you say? What is this, a rite of passage? Yes it is.

Verlaine – is there something you wish to do, my man, Verlaine? Is there a reddish hue on your head you wish to curtail? And when we are through, there comes a nightingale truce, something that leads the nowhere to the somewhere.

Heavy handed, and moist to the touch – there are brims full, and chestnuts open. Be the weather, it will suit your hand. Be the weather, and the weather will come for you. Be the marks on the rock, and the rockfish will not startle.

Verlaine – Open to the sound, the sound of ages. Beginning just a little bit at a time. We feel landfall, and have it raise us to the top once more. In the distance we see the chains that bind, but we have seen them so soon, we can negotiate passage.

Having never seen a day like this, we wander through art galleries, that stand in disused buildings, and adjust the timings of things to account of the daylight. And then, a new insistence beckons – we will follow it to where it wants to go.

Verlaine – the need we have to settle old scores. One, in the middle, two, through the height, three, and then go. There is mischief here, like a well-known feat. We are inclined at this point to rally for a further assault. We will come, and come again.

Hearing that something special, I no longer doubt myself. It is here, in the chosen field, where I used to play as a child, I see the footfalls of life, and then the red of the clay, and know life to be precious. There is something more here, but what?

Verlaine – the stomping ground is precious, and more than that, much more. I will see you at the park. I will see you in the sky, and then turn around.

New seasons always bring the rain. New temperatures never stall what comes next. There are phases of the moon that do not come close. There are people who never need to say. There are folk that have as their repartee the dimensions of the sun.

Verlaine – have you the hearth, and the dream-like abandon? Is yours the whetstone up against it? Do you stall in the face of the sense of things? Are we apt to call our home a home? Do we disguise ourselves in pieces of twine, never to be seen?

Hauling the last of it, up a big rise. There is more than we can tell. What is there left though? What is there left, to gather up like rose petals? We know what is best, but what of this? We come for a dime, and settle for a shilling. Come and take a seat.

Verlaine – is this where we are at? Is this the time it takes to settle old scores, and loosen old wounds. I can write like no other, but that should settle you. There are places that let in the breeze, and these places are blessed, for now at least.

Catching the sunlight. Catching the grey of it, and the aqua, and the steel. Yes the sunlight has steel. It travels long distances, and knows not when to stop. For this purpose it must have steel. And when it is no more, it keeps going, in different guises

Verlaine – incessant, and alive. Coming close to the edge of something we don't understand. Forever listening, and hoping, forever alive, and willing. We have a thought that never lets be. Never folds, never relinquishes. Never.

There is a chest, that contains the whole world. And in that chest, and in this world, is some-thing special. Not something to throw away, but to let be, and harvest when the time is right. And this thing is the water of things – the water in the womb!

Verlaine – this is what I am looking for! Do you come Verlaine, when things are precious? When things are in bloom – do you come? From your vantage in the sky? Do you come, where excellences beckon, much like Rimbaud!

Gracious, and at ease, we see ourselves right in the middle of it, and give our applause, not from afar, as you might expect, but from a distance becoming the suitor and the chased. There is now a wish had by everyone – to still, and breathe.

Verlaine – what is it you seek, my Verlaine? What time of day do you arise, and then sleep? There are cornices worth doing, and doing well. There are nuances to fate that we can hardly tell of – this much is true! What have we felt then, but all.

Sleeping through it all, we lounge once again on the side-glimpses of hope that have had their fill for so long. There are tantrums in the sand that do not carry any weight. There are things we do that we shouldn't, but that is okay – never to see.

PAUL VERLAINE

Verlaine – giving our all, for love and purpose. Giving what we need to come full circle. I have found a way, through the detritus, and the willow shed, to build a new world, one with no er-rors, and no need to set sail to any other place.

Missing that something else, I am in full command of my potential. I have risen to new heights, and have sailed down the river of fate, with hands out held.

Verlaine – are you alive? Do you have wings, and can fly? I believe in you, my strange stranger, I believe in your power to overcome, which is nothing but a steel and a shovel. Do not linger, it will hurt. Do not stop the way of it, you will see.

Foraging for the right to stand tall in a basin made of clay, and a simplicity made of desire. What is this thing called love? Can it lend a helping hand? Can it be all that it should be? There is nothing that can suffice. All that is left is left.

Verlaine – opening the doors, do you see the place we do? Do you sense the charms of dis-placement that hold in track the very fibres of the soul. Come and be a part of it. This thing called life, will never end, and luck would have it, never began.

Gauging in the tempest mount, there is a place more fully formed than we would have hoped. The belief we have, is the same belief that we have always had. What's more, the ticklish and the fire breathing are never too close. We come and go.

Verlaine – The mystery of it, is surmountable, in time, we will see it through, and know our-selves to be wondrous. That we see ourselves now at all, is a once off thing. That we have the load, and the load has us, is a miracle of proportions.

Simply being, and setting up watch, knowing there will be more to come, and more in store than ever. I sincerely hope you are through, because we cannot go through that again. We are through, and for that matter, home.

Verlaine – are you king of your own castle? Do you love the way you are? Is this the way of it, through, and under? Can we settle back down again, and know life to be something we must muster – muster in time to be? Come, we will away.

Simple things, things cared for. Things to vanquish, things to help. There is like a right course, amongst the ways of it, and here, much is said, and much unsaid. The truly tiresome does not inflict here, only sees through, and moves on.

Verlaine – conscious of the way, we spark another fire. I think in passing it will suffice to herald another day. Forever seeing, forever upright, never dancing on heightened flames. What is there left? What can there be now? What has there been then?

Harrowing, and in need of water. There is like a thousand new barbs upon the waking of the day. A thousand new barbs, that come and go through out the rest of the day. But what do we have of them, now that they shimmer – are they gone?

Verlaine – a languorous endeavour. One that lets the land fall come, and be as it may. There are side stepped hopes, and mistletoe coats. And things to catch by, and never evoke a stand. Things to reach for, and things to drown out. Yes, much fun.

Swift, and yet with trepidation. There is enough to bolster any ridge. And then, without as much as a care, there resounds a mighty sound, one that has the trees bending for breath. There is here, a thing that cannot stop. We will watch it.

Verlaine – I see things clearly now, and have done for the last few days. There are things in me I cannot explain, but have now passed, and have settled.

Gasping, and gnashing and coming up for air. There is never a time like this. There is always a time like this. The gloom, erodes the doubt, as the light begins to shine. There is nothing like this now! We have come, and let us sample the rain!

Verlaine – are you one to sleep past eleven in the morning? Or when is it that you wake? It matters little, we are just eager to know. Sometimes are like the wheel of fate, and sometimes are for the more adventurous! Are you up, Verlaine?

Seeing things as they are, not as they should be. There is a reverberation through the hive, that sparks a wanton cry. Do come with me, my creed, do come, there will be a time for laugh-ter here, laughter and belief, laughter and solitude.

Verlaine – are you full of life, where you are? Do you sing the loudest when you can, and have full voice? Is this what you have come to say – I am here, like the whistle stop that hardens no arches, and gives rise to the error of the plains.

Driving the last carriage through the wind, through the rain. There is a place in amongst it, that has no name, no face, nor any enjambment. There are things we must do here, things we must say. To give respite the weary – tally forth.

Verlaine – There are weddings that are eager for their recompense. And there are weddings that style themselves on the blessings to come. There are now two things to do! One, hatch a solemn desire, and two, have it sprout up.

Maybe wishing too soon? Well, never too late. There are things we do, that have as the crust of it more than anything in this life. And here, where the marrow is shucked, there comes a new time to dance, and dance afresh. Come now, do not ponder.

Verlaine – offset by the beat of drums, there is a nice-time to remonstrate, and remonstrate dearly. Have the forest of the moon come, and shimmy down the ledges of all that is. I sense your needing to be, but I don't wish to impede.

Going for a walk, and never coming back. Going for something, and releasing all that is. A sense that the time is a shallow dish, and a wanting that has itself more to give than to holler. A fishing that has no life to stand. That is the end of it.

Verlaine – never missing a beat. Always coming that extra distance. Also doing the accepting, and the rite of passages. Do not sing here, to do so wrecks the scene. Have a hallowed waste bin, and never let it fill. And there we have it!

Thinking things through, we should rush at it with a receptacle, and never let it stray. There are times that do not disagree with us. There are times that do. Do not belittle the stranger – he is here for good tidings. We will rush at the rest.

Verlaine – much older now, in the blink of a stage. Much wiser, but less fun. Much in the way of things, but do we

tout? Do we have those things again we had in childhood.
No, we have chosen a path, and let us stick to it.

Gaining a foothold, we relinquish our grip. And here, like a
coaster train, there remains all of us to say, 'time!' Come
now, we must not sense.

Verlaine – do you weep? Are you in anger? Do the things
you do fall from places of height? Is this the way we stand?
Never letting go, never wincing from afar. The noise of the
distance does not bother us, but that of closer up, catches.

Kicking the dust, through sands of the hourglass. There is
something here we do not under-stand. I have reached far
for this, and know I am solidly evoked. Do not bend a knee,
the tres-tle is already set. And then, an afterthought, decree?

Verlaine – are you away, with sport, as in life? Does your tail
bight, and not together? There are people at the bridge, we
will find them. And here, where the sails of distaste do not
linger, there is a marching that comes of age, and then,
sport.

Actually, there is a time for this place. There is a nuance that
knows only grace. And then, with the things forgotten, there
comes a new need to be, and also be wary. Come now, we
must not be shy, there are edges that sense only the
embrace.

Verlaine – aching to deliver the seeds, we find the distance
of the laity something we must not watch. And then, the
stupor of the fished for diatribe, is not in wonderment (any
more than is usual), there comes a sound we cannot forget.

Branching out, we see ourselves in fibrous attire, and then, when we are amongst it, we trade our clothes for others. The collar is high, and the tails are long. And now, and then, we find ourselves with things to say, and things to do.

Verlaine – seeing the harp, but not wanting to play. Seeing what is next, and doing a little dance. Having a near miss, but returning to the fold. There are things we must not remember, and things we must. And here, a new line of thought. Come, anon.

Further than we ever thought possible. Further than the round has ever gone. And then, with-out a need, nor avarice, nor things to see, we send our ships down mighty channels, to do what they do best. And here, a new set of parameters to measure.

Verlaine – do you sense the ease of the way? Do you keep going no matter what? Is that what we have at hand, and only that? There are things we must not keep, and things we must wrestle to the ground. All the more tendency to laugh!

Having what is needed, and then being off. Doing what the map says, and making it through. Treasuring things like never before. Only what we can take with us. And then, a caste rotunda, gives something special to the scene. It will last.

Verlaine – are these things of value to you? Are the meanderings of fate what we need? I have sensed something new for a while now, and maybe now we have something fresh. Do not begin from here. But listen, there is time.

Having the sense unbroken, that is what we want. And then, where we linger nightly, there is a passage that hears itself in further hues. Never again will we send the ships unto the rudder. Never again, will we find ourselves with something gone.

Verlaine – do you see what I do Verlaine? Do you manage on your own? Through times of unbidden joy? This is what we want – to see the stanzas through the glass.

Having a load made easy. Having what comes next! Being like the shadow, but not knowing when to burn. The distress of it, comes thick. The walk is nothing we should contemplate, but we do anyway. In the sense of it there is a gale.

Verlaine – managing as best we can, without recourse to the wind. There are places here, we have dreamt of, but they are not the ones for us. Our dreams are of further cycles, and more solid things. We will not linger, but neither waste.

Only going that one step at a time. There are missions that herald embarking calls. There are things that have as their arrows the flights of eagles. And then, when the moss speaks, there comes a new found belief, that grows as the daylight.

Verlaine – come now, do not be thick. Do not be the queen below the edges, nor the duck be-neath the snow. I am here to deliver, and deliver I will. There are things we must not see, and things we have already seen. But do not tally forth.

Gaining in shoulder width, we see ourselves come anew. There are things that have harboured regrets as a polished stone. Do not see these things again. Because when the night comes, it really comes at full velocity. Shirk not, we see you.

Verlaine – never like a tumbling mass, that feeds in cycles of the dawn. Never seeing what we must, and, then, only what we need. There are chances all bright as the rainbow. Let us see this thing, and have an unruly time of it. Please come.

Harbouring nothing of regret. Seeing the withering on the vine, and knowing it won't last. There are things we must only do at the break of dawn. And here, where there is not a thing to do, we will gather ourselves for one last dusk.

Verlaine – where are you? Where is your soul, it is deep. Deep within. There are constants, and there are fluctuating things. What is fluctuating is for the life of the sparrows, the constants, the life of the mare. Do we call it even!

Dreaming, like never before. Dreaming large, dreaming small, dreaming in-between. Our dreams are what sustains us. And here, where the time is like a new born, the trumpeting of the score allows no rest. Do not come here, we will fly.

Verlaine – have we cast ourselves in bronze? Have we cast ourselves in wannabe blue? And then, with aplomb, and side-glimpsed hope, there is a missive from the beyond. It reads – "Thankyou sir/madam for your help with our garden…"

Gracious in wanting to do more. Gracious in not wanting to do less. There is a symmetry here, that does not belie the tale. Come now, we must away, if only for a brief time, a brief time in the sun. Do not size up the fairy cloth. It is best left.

Verlaine – are you the one to walk, from here to there, and back again? Are you the one to seal our fate with a kiss? Do the ramparts sing of your name, still? What is this thing you want? This thing that sings in tune? We will come, maybe tomorrow.

Feathers that know no weight. That know only height. Believe in us, dear one, believe in the wayfarer, as is their delight. Sense more than we ever have.

Verlaine, are you eloping? Do you see the time? Is this just a ransom, to be paid at the hour? Are you leaving – please come! Do you sense the friendship at hand? Come now, forever is upon us. Do not straddle the vine, it is made of sterner stuff.

Raging, and in sync. The life we have invigorates, and tires, in equal measure. We wish we had the key, to unlock the mighty and the down trodden. There are times of sweetest bliss, and the times of unbridled care. Be with us that one last time!

Verlaine – casting forth, and then seeing the window range through. There are nuances to the hearing we have, that say to us, here, and, there. Do not be surprised, there are ways through the maze, come and see. Come and see.

Hanging on, for the life of it. Hanging on, for the dearest. There are travels that must be at-tained, and then not forgotten. We are here, before the gates. We are here, before the planes. Where is the summit – over here I say. Over where? Over here.

Verlaine – A mighty hand, that comes in the way of it. Do not be surprised, we have come. The night is like a wholesome embrace, that heralds as it decries. There is lasting anguish here, like a bird swept to its own heaven. Be like a beauty.

Feeling like the sense we have in the way forward. Feeling like things that never sleep. And here there are nuances that are tidy, and some that are dense. I will never doubt you. I say this in my sleep. And then, a catching sound, and through.

Verlaine, do you sense your own name? Is this the way to go? Abbreviated and indelible. Catch us something we can throw back, and let live. Be the show, and yours will be your fill. There are turns that do not fathom. Come with us!

Jettisoning the night lamp. Its glow is too comforting, and too bewildering. We now must have something else. We will find it, as we least expect it. And here where love and frivolity give away in everyday care. Come now, there is a time.

Verlaine, do you care? Do you willow the range, in search of puddles? Do you sink once again into quicksand? Is there anything you can do? Don't worry, we will find you again. We will find you, and see you once again. Do not worry.

Missing, with features unbridled. And then, when two score years and ten are upon us, we will shout for more, and give less. What is the thing worth searching for? What is this thing known to us? I am like the buzzard, carefree.

Verlaine – are you a sense amongst the nonsense? Are you a tired rat amongst the trees? Do you stampede with gusto and gumption? Is this the way we proceed? It must be the way of it, and so forth. I catch on a tree, oh me! And now…

Kings and queens, we know not which is which! And here for a time, we will rest our heads, and know the flame to be the bringer of truth. There can only be that which is not enough.

That which is free is another matter. Do not placate me, I am learning.

Verlaine – Do you taste of things differently now? Do you wander near and far? Is this the way to see? Are we here, where we want to be? Yes, and yes.

Nestling in close, there seems a little way to go. And now, now that we have no more of a shoulder to cry on, we should not relinquish the score, for anybody, not anyone. Without the light, there cannot be the tailor. Without the simplicity, nothing.

Verlaine – are you conscious of much needed rain? Does the new tethering on old flames count for much? Are we the ones that have not the accoutrement? Caught in the in-between of things, there is a cry, then nothing! What we would give.

Coming back to the middle of things. Never trying too hard. Never being one to dismiss. There are rangers that do not tire. There are things we must not do. Holding on, we favour the dis-tance and the might. This much is how we want to be.

Verlaine – catching the train at speed. Having nothing else to tell of. While we gain speed, something else arises. We cannot tell what is next. We cannot tell. And then, when the night is at its peak, a new shambles to come down from.

Do you know what the stars say? Do you know what ingenious plans are here? The truth of it beckons. Do not dismiss us, we are, for some, reality. A measure of persistence, and then, crescendo. Be a favourable mention in a house of cards.

Verlaine – Are you the one to speak? Do you come in glimpses of sand and ice? Is this the way we slumber? On beds of rose petals, on beds of irises. We come, not in the morning, but for the night. And here, much sparked for conversation.

And then, and almighty crash. What is it? What is that sound? It is more than we can cope with. I have sensed the sand in the hour glass, not seeming a thing. Do not be surprised at things, they are quick. Quick as the road upon which we walk.

Verlaine – do you see yourself as the wandering of autumnal fireflies? Is this what the rouse is? I have no time to bungle on the bridge. No time to see what is real. I have said before, there is no time to believe in the dusk, unless...

Very fine, and very upright, the disk of flame has not what the dance of the December moon has in store. What is that we feed on, silk and wild-berries? There is something near our own hearts, that we cannot dismiss with anger and frivolity.

Verlaine – have me now, oh one of the hill. Have the ripeness of two veins. Love the place we are at! Love the chimes as they beckon. Love the moisture of the plains. The tassel of the clo-sure is now. Come, we must only seek. And seek again.

Voyaging through the mist, the hills depart, and come again in rays of light. We have come to invigorate, and to shake hands with fate. There is a price to be paid, and that is your counte-nance. We will send again through the hour, and then!

Verlaine – tip top, as the spire in the wind. What do you have for us? What has the Sunday charm never said to us? What has the sail in consummate wind never failed to do? I will never come to rouse, only to say, I will. Disaffected and whispering.

Vestiges of what lies ahead. A sign so large it bends under its own weight. And now, what we most have sought for - the talons of absentia. Come now; yes.

Verlaine, the best of it, and the worst. Come now, do not be surprised. Do not do that thing that is for scoundrels, and wanton men. We have a better plan is store. I see you slithering, on the ground, like snake in the grass. Do not bend, you will break.

A buttress to our soul, is what we need. There can only be the staring of large fields, otherwise. The mischief in the trees is here. And then, do you know what, more than enough. We are gruesome in our attire. But it is our best! Yes, we know!

Verlaine – have you seen the wilderness, Verlaine? Maybe during your farming escapade? Yes but what of it? Just wanting to know, and for the forest to lap you in. There is nothing so tolerable as an adventure, every now and then, don't you think?

Holding to great force. Is there a time requirement here, I ask? There is now a sense of thinks come harking. We will not hold you back, so go and have your fun. Do not play mischief in the seed and the wandering of things. We will come, to let go.

Verlaine – do you wash your hands, again? Do you feel life is at the cross-roads? Is there more time than is hirsute? Do the tangles of a worn out place come to gag you? Is this where we are from? From the back of it – looking forward?

Verlaine – this is where we are at, in the lens, looking towards the sky? Do you follow suit without the need to tailor. There is something gratuitous here, and we don't know what. Oh well, it will be fun, nevertheless. Come forward, great one.

Avast, and alive! Get to know the semblance of things. Get to know adventures that have no end. Be the top of the bastion, as it sails. Have more than we can expect. And then, with the thorn in the balance, strike, and have our fill.

Verlaine – do you serve the right amount of delight? Is that where we turn? I have found you in the metropolis, and you only. What is this thing we do, that others do not? I do not know, but will find out. Please let me in from the cold!

I have a vested interest in the soul to soul search, of them some, and then only. What is this we seek? What toil do we find here? There is a magic to this place that cannot be replicated. Sing now, there is nothing further.

Verlaine – have you come to conquer? Have you come to raise a sail? Do not believe in things here, there is much of a muchness. And when we find the way, we will tell all, and through the fibres of things, we will laugh!

Forgetting the ground beneath our feet. Forgetting, the sand between our toes. There is a time, and a place, for every last song. Do not take away our silence, we need that to live. And then, without the slightest care, anon!

PAUL VERLAINE

Verlaine – there are times that heed a drum, and times that don't. Everything we need is here. And then, despite acceptances, a dial on the return. A shift, and without need, a new type of desire, one that gives as well as takes.

Having time for the restless, and not being accepting of the loss. And now, despite ourselves, a hard won belief, throwing all that is, on top of, all that is.

Verlaine – whispers in the night. A silence too large to engulf. What is this I hear you say? Never abroad, only to stay. Forgetting the wind, that seeing is ripe. We are here, here to say more. There is time to be once again. Time to be.

Gaining courage from it. Hearing what it is worth. It is worth a hundred gales of wind, that stipulates more from the soil. Now and then we fight, but only for the crusts. Have you seen the way of it? I have. And what did you think? A lot.

Verlaine – are you the one? Verlaine, do you see? Do you see where others can't? There is a ransom in this, that spoils no fruit. Come to the setting with aplomb, give moisture where it is due, and then come, come again.

I think of things often, and know not where to turn. There is a metaphysical angst here, my Verlaine. But what of it? Surely there are more important things happening – of course. But we must survive. And that we do, but of life?

Verlaine – question me! Question me quickly! Are we resolved to stay where we are? Does time envision us to stay calm. We are sporting batons of clay. We will win every fight, every last one. There is no turning back. None.

Catching a hold, there is life, there is strength, there is tiredness, and apathy. But we will not give in. We cannot. It is up and over, every time. And here where I see things more deeply, I know the test comes in multiple ways. And so, we live for it.

Verlaine – casting out the surge, and having time to remember. There are things and places that know no time, and have a lapse in the corridors of it. Down to section B, and across the lope to a new kind of place. Never found, always looked for.

Crossing the pastures, we see well. What have we found now, but the windswept and the congealed? There can only be what is here, nothing more than captures. What we see, is the most we can, given the circumstances. Some will change.

Verlaine – hoping for the best, expecting things to swarm. What is it that we hold here? What is it that we hold, and cannot let go of? It is life, and all sorts of rungs, and tidy pieces of news. Can we ever see the way? Of course!

Very straight, this road. Very straight, with lopsided fences. The houses sit perpendicular, but what of the line of trees? We see them sit, and hang in front of us. There are things we do not understand here. We will wait. And see what comes.

Verlaine - there are noisy wheels here, but the horses that drive them? Nowhere to be seen. The carriage? Steeped in mist. What can we do to stave off the rails? We can loom large in the face of it. Do not be a tempter in a tempters yard.

The very next day! And what of that? Do we see ourselves again through marshes and into climes? Into wells, and through again. There are vaults, vaults that temper. Never do we reign the words down from the heights. We must wait.

Verlaine – do you see the train coming? Are you waiting for Rimbaud? Do you see the steam of the train, is it coming your way? Distance, and the spice of existence.

Lost in footfall. Never righting the circle. Never seeing into things, but always sensing. Always doing, and always saying. We have lost a lark, that comes our way, from time to time. There is never anything more we can do. Nothing more to say.

Verlaine – And here, where we faint the most. There is time to be had, on both sides. Never before have we had the wayfarer come, in locks of gold, locks of sheet. There is now a tendril, lost on gauges, lost on weirs. Do not hesitate, and then rush!

Accosting on the way of it. Leaving too soon. There is merriment in the wind, and we see it. Conscious of the plateau, we dive again, and see ourselves float by. Running into water, run-ning into air. There is time for both, and both impending.

Verlaine – are you the which-way now. Please bend a signal for the dawn, and believe it to be true. There are things we must delight in, and things that require temperance. Does the spring liken itself to the fisher and the mandibles?

Wrestling free of the sand, we come again to that extra mile, that knows its grace, and shades of want. Do we see ourselves once again in turns of steel, turns of love. We no longer see ourselves as we were. We only see what is next.

Verlaine – alcoves and intransigence. Night-time skies. What was once the harvest, is now the fisher of contemplation. There is a place beyond all places. And we have found the key. Never lost in the motion of it, never too dry. Always on the face of it.

"For he was weak in all things, except poetic creation!"

Readers Note

The structure of this book follows the trajectory of Verlaine's poetic career. Can you tell how?